PARABLES FOR PERSONAL GROWTH

Tales for Your Healing Journey

MELINDA REINICKE

o   o   o

RECOVERY PUBLICATIONS, INC.

SAN DIEGO

Published by Recovery Publications, Inc.
1201 Knoxville Street
San Diego, CA 92110
(619) 275-1350

Library of Congress Cataloging-in-Publication Data
Reinicke, Melinda, 1956–
Parables for personal growth : tales for your healing journey /
Melinda Reinicke. — 1st ed.
p.   cm.
Includes bibliographical references.
ISBN 0-941405-22-2
1. Parables—Therapeutic use.   2. Self-help techniques.
I. Title.
RC489.F3R45   1993
158'.1—dc20   92-42688
                    CIP

Printed in the United States of America
First edition
10 9 8 7 6 5 4 3 2 1

TO THOSE WHO STRUGGLE AGAINST

DRAGONS AND DARKNESS

o   o   o

CONTENTS

○ ○ ○

○   ○   ○

ACKNOWLEDGMENTS

○   ○   ○

WITH THANKS

To RON HALVORSON and VALERIE DEILGAT of Recovery Publications, who fell in love with the parables and made a dream come true for me.

To JAN JOHNSON, my editor, for her valuable input and to BRAD SARGENT for his generous help on the book proposal.

To JEAN GRAHAM and NOREEN CULLENWARD for their encouragement on the original manuscript.

To MARIBETH EKEY and ROZ BURSIK for treasured friendship and heartfelt prayers through tough times and celebrations.

To MY CLIENTS, courageous travelers, who have allowed me to walk beside them when their paths were difficult.

To PAT and GAIL PEACOCK, my parents, who gave me a magical childhood and watched their grandson, NATHAN, extra hours while I wrote this book.

To AARON, who did not think my secret passion for writing was foolish and birthed this book by asking me for a parable to use in one of his seminars. He is a kind and handsome prince with whom I always want to live happily ever after.

Most of all, to the GREAT KING who helps me in the struggle against the dragons, trolls, and ogres in my life. His land is, indeed, a wondrous place.

TAKING A JOURNEY WITH THE PARABLES

o   o   o

*I*n a mythical realm not far from your own inner struggles, you will find travelers in these pages who join you on your sojourn. A noble prince who falls under the sway of a destructive dragon allows you to feel the process of recovery from self-defeating behavior. In another parable, an enchanted mirror leads a princess to mistakenly believe she is grotesque. Eventually she discovers her true identity.

These parables not only help us see our wounds, but they also show us how to mend that brokenness. Something about a parable whispers to our hearts and helps us embrace truth into our lives. We feel the emotions of the story, we grasp the difficulty of the road ahead, and we carry with us the pictures of the parable to help us in the choices we face.

Written for adults on a personal growth journey, the parables speak to the heart as well as the mind. Self-defeating behavior, codependency, inner child work, boundaries, depression, self-concept, loss of childhood, recovery from childhood abuse, dysfunctional family interactions, fears, anxiety, unhealthy group victimization, forgiving and letting go, loss and grief: many of these apply, if not to you, then to someone you love. Even issues that may, on the surface, have nothing to do with you, carry parallels in your own life. Your dragon may not be addictive or compulsive, but you know the talons of self-defeating behavior. Your uncle may not have danced with you in the dark, but you have felt betrayed by someone you loved.

Similarly, the gender of the main characters is varied, but the truths apply equally to either sex. There are many male codependents, many women who were the angry scapegoats in their families, and many men who were molested as children.

The parables are particularly useful in opening feelings that have been closed off. So ask yourself as you experience the parable, "What am I feeling? What part of the story brought this feeling? What is the parallel in my own life?"

A section for personal reflection follows each parable. These pages involve you through writing, drawing, imagining, meditating, and other experiences designed to lead you toward more wholeness in your life. Feel free to skip exercises you don't feel ready for. And, if at any time you feel overwhelmed by memories or emotions sparked by a parable, please talk to a good friend or counselor.

Since any journey is better with company, you might consider going through the parables with a friend, Twelve-Step sponsor, or support group. The book lends itself to either individual journaling or group exploration. For those wanting more information on group use, please see Appendix 1, page 171.

You may be an avid reader of recovery or self-help books, but the parables will reach a part of you that lecture-style books did not. Or, perhaps you don't enjoy reading and aren't familiar with recovery principles. The parables will refreshingly introduce you to personal growth without boring or overloading you with "psychologese."

You may be a new traveler, only recently having discovered the road to wholeness. You are eager to learn what is ahead and how to get there. Others of you may be seasoned travelers, but would appreciate some encouragement on the long trek. It is, after all, a never-ending journey. The longer we travel, the stronger our injured souls become, the fewer pitfalls we stumble into, the more beauty we notice around us. May these parables help you enjoy your own wondrous sojourn.

In a mythical realm not far from your own inner struggles . . .

THE DRAGON

o o o

There was once a great and noble King whose land was terrorized by a crafty dragon. Like a massive bird of prey the scaly beast delighted in ravaging villages with his fiery breath. Hapless victims ran from their burning homes only to be snatched into the dragon's jaws or talons. Those devoured instantly were deemed more fortunate than those carried back to the dragon's lair to be devoured at his leisure.

The King led his sons and knights in many valiant battles against the serpent. Each time they wounded the dragon, and he retreated to his hidden lair deep in the mountains. While he healed, the kingdom would be at peace for a time. "Take courage," the King told his people. "One day the dragon will be slain."

Riding alone in the forest during a period of calm, one of the King's sons heard his name purred low and soft. In the shadows of the ferns and trees, curled among the boulders, lay the dragon. The creature's heavy-lidded eyes fastened on the prince, and the reptilian mouth stretched into a friendly smile.

"Don't be alarmed," said the dragon as gray wisps of smoke rose lazily from his nostrils. "I am not what your father thinks."

"What are you, then?" asked the prince, warily drawing his sword as he pulled in the reins to keep his fearful horse from bolting.

"I am pleasure," said the dragon. "Ride on my back and you will experience more than you ever imagined. Come now. I have no harmful intentions. I seek a friend, someone to share flights with me. Have you never dreamed of flying? Never longed to soar in the clouds?" The sunlight glistened with an iridescent sheen on the dragon's metallic green scales. "Bring your sword for security if you wish, but I give my word no harm will come to you."

Visions of soaring high above the forested hills drew the prince hesitantly from his horse. The dragon unfurled one great webbed wing to serve as a ramp to his ridged back. Between the spiny projections, the prince found a secure seat. Then the creature snapped his powerful wings twice and launched them into the sky. Once aloft the dragon wafted effortlessly on the wind streams. The prince's apprehension melted into awe and exhilaration.

From then on, he met the dragon often, but secretly, for how could he tell his father, brothers, or the knights that he had befriended the enemy? The prince felt separate from them all. Their concerns were no longer his concerns. Even when he wasn't with the dragon he spent less time with those he loved and more time alone.

The skin on the prince's legs became calloused from gripping the ridged back of the dragon, and his hands grew rough and hardened. He began wearing gloves to hide the malady. After many nights of riding, he discovered scales growing on the backs of his hands as well. With dread he realized his fate were he to continue, and so he resolved to return no more to the dragon.

But, after a fortnight, he again sought out the dragon, having been tortured with desire. And so it transpired many times over. No matter what his determination, the prince eventually found himself pulled back, as if by the cords of an invisible web. Silently, patiently, the dragon always waited.

One cold, moonless night their excursion became a foray against a sleeping village. Torching the thatched roofs with fiery blasts from his nostrils, the dragon roared with delight when terrified victims fled from their burning homes. Swooping in, the serpent belched again and flames engulfed a cluster of screaming villagers. The prince closed his eyes tightly in an attempt to shut out the carnage, but the agonized cries and smell of burning flesh assailed him. The dragon's long neck snaked and spasmed as he crunched bone and devoured his roasted prey. The prince retched and clung miserably to his spiny perch.

In the predawn hours, when the prince crept back from his dragon trysts, the road outside his father's castle usually remained empty. But, not tonight. Terrified refugees streamed into the protective walls of the castle. The prince walked among bedraggled women carrying wailing children with gashes from the dragon's talons. Some victims, too badly wounded or burned to walk, were brought in carts or dragged on makeshift pallets.

The prince's heart was torn. Their pain brought tears to his eyes and shame to his soul. "What have I become?" he asked himself. At that moment, he wanted even more desperately to be free of the dragon. Perhaps his father, in all his wisdom, could help. But the prince feared that the truth would make him abhorrent in his father's sight. Surely he would be disowned, exiled, or perhaps even condemned to death.

The castle bustled with frantic activity as people rushed about to care for the refugees that thronged in the courtyard. The prince attempted to slip through the crowd to close himself in his chambers, but some of the survivors stared and pointed toward him.

"He was there," one woman cried out, "I saw him on the back of the dragon." Others nodded their heads in angry agreement. Horrified, the prince saw that his father, the King, was in the courtyard holding a bleeding child in his arms. The King's face mirrored the agony of his people as his eyes found the prince's. The son fled, hoping to escape into the night, but the guards apprehended him as if he were a common thief. They brought him to the great hall where his father sat solemnly on the throne. The people on every side railed against the prince.

"Banish him!" he heard one of his own brothers angrily cry out.

"Flay him!"

"Burn him alive!" other voices shouted.

As the King rose from his throne, bloodstains from the wounded shone darkly on his royal robes. The crowd fell silent in expectation of his decree. The prince, who could not bear to look into his father's face, stared at the flagstones of the floor.

"Take off your gloves and your tunic," the King commanded. The prince obeyed slowly, dreading to have his metamorphosis uncovered before the kingdom. Was his shame not already great enough? He had hoped for a quick death without further humiliation. Sounds of revulsion rippled through the crowd at the sight of the prince's thick, scaled skin and the ridge growing along his spine.

The King strode toward his son and the prince steeled himself, fully expecting a back-handed blow even though he had never been struck so by his father.

Instead, his father embraced him and wept as he held him tightly. In shocked disbelief, the prince buried his face against his father's shoulder.

"Do you wish to be freed of the dragon, my son?"

The prince answered in despair, "I have wished it many times, but there is no hope for me."

"Not alone," said the King. "You cannot win against the serpent alone."

"Father, I am no longer your son. I am half beast," sobbed the prince.

But his father replied, "My blood runs in your veins. My nobility has always been stamped deep within your soul. Nothing can take that from you."

With his face still hidden tearfully in his father's embrace, the prince heard the King instruct the crowd, "The dragon is crafty. Some fall victim to his wiles and some to his violence. There will be mercy for all who wish to be freed. Who else among you has ridden the dragon?"

The prince lifted his head to see someone emerge from the crowd. To his amazement, he recognized an older brother, one who had been lauded throughout the kingdom for his onslaughts against the dragon in battle and for his many good deeds. Others came, some weeping, others hanging their heads in shame. The sister who was known for her beautiful singing came, tearfully removing her slippers to reveal spiked scales on her feet.

The King embraced them all.

"This is our most powerful weapon against the dragon," he announced. "Truth. No more hidden flights. Alone you cannot resist him. Together you will prevail, for you draw strength from one another. Those of you who think yourselves immune to the serpent's wiles, beware lest you be the next to fall. Those ensnared, you must desire freedom more than the dragon's flight. The struggle will be long and fierce. Over time, you will choose more often against the dragon than for him until finally you go to him no more."

"Will the scales then be gone as well?" asked the sister, looking at her bared feet.

"No, my child," the King answered gently. "But, in time, they will fade. And one day, when the dragon is finally slain, all traces of the scales will disappear."

"Death to the dragon!" someone yelled from the crowd, and a great cheer rose up in chorus, "Death to the dragon! Long live the King!"

○　　　○　　　○

Personal Reflection

The Dragon

✎ Parts of the parable that touched me are . . .

✎ When I read these parts I felt . . .

✎ Similar situations in my life are . . .

We all struggle with self-defeating behaviors that ensnare us like a crafty dragon. In the space below, draw two pictures. Don't worry about artistic ability. Simply draw freely as you did when you were a child.

Myself in the Shadow of the Dragon   *Myself Freed from the Dragon*

What scales and scars do you try to hide from others? _____
_____
_____

What would your life be like without the dragon? _____
_____
_____

Trusting My Higher Power: The prince mistakenly believed that the King would punish him. If my Higher Power seems harsh, I can replace that view by picturing the compassionate King in the story. To get to know my Higher Power better I can . . .

✍ _____
_____
_____
_____

LADY IN WAITING

o   o   o

*A*n exuberant throng greeted the returning knights. The dragon
had been sorely wounded. There would be peace in the land while the creature
hid deep in his lair and licked his wounds. Although battered, torn, and
scorched, the knights had taken no mortal blows, but one mighty steed was
lost to the dragon's jaws. Stirred by the excitement of the people, the tired war
horses stomped and snorted in the courtyard as their riders dismounted. Pages
scurried to remove their lords' armor.

The princess moved through the crowd helping the women dress wounds,
for she was known throughout the land for her skill in the ancient healing arts.
Knowledge of medicinal herbs had been passed like a legacy from generation
to generation in her mother's family. Thinking that all were attended, she was
leaving to oversee preparations for the celebration feast, when her eyes fell on
a hastily wrapped bandage around one knight's hand.

"No one has seen to your injury," she apologized setting down her basket
of herbs and dressings beside him.

"There are others more in need of care," he said.

"They are being tended," she insisted and reached for his arm, but he
moved it away. He was a stranger to her, one of the knights sent by the Great
King to help her father's men fight against the dragon.

"Come now," she chided, thinking he was a typical warrior who fought
bravely in battle only to run from the sting of ointments.

"I tended it myself," he explained.

Not dissuaded, she grasped his arm firmly to unwrap the blood-soaked cloth from his hand. But the skin revealed when she unwound the wrap caused her to pause. The gash in his hand cut across crusty, hardened scales.

So this was one of the Great King's sons who had been beguiled into riding the dragon. She had heard stories about the scandal: how those lured to fly on the dragon became more beast-like with each secret rendezvous; how the King had pardoned all those so ensnared; how they valiantly struggled to eschew the dragon and battle him wherever they might.

Silently, she lifted a cask of water to rinse the wound and then applied ointment. Now she understood his reluctance to accept her ministration. She could only guess at the shame he carried. Wrapping a clean bandage in place, she ventured a look into his unmarred face. It was a handsome face with kind eyes. For an instant she saw gratitude there, but then his countenance suddenly flashed to anger and he took his leave speedily.

During the evening's festivities, the princess felt quite sure he avoided her. Whenever she looked in his direction, he turned away. Unaccustomed to such curt behavior, and wondering how she had offended him, the princess resolved to speak to him directly. The next day she sent a servant to request his presence as she sat in the garden weaving a tapestry on her loom.

"My Lady," he greeted her politely but without warmth.

"Good Prince," she acknowledged him, and they walked a short distance from her attendants. "You are an abrupt man, my lord," she stated without malice. "What have I done to be treated so unkindly?"

"How have I been unkind, good Lady?" he inquired guardedly.

"You have avoided me and had no company with me at the banquet."

"You would wish to company with me?" he asked.

"Who would not wish to befriend a knight so noble and brave?"

"And scaled." The prince watched for her reaction, but she was unruffled.

"The scales are only further evidence of your courage. I have heard that the battle to leave off dragon flights is the hardest battle of all."

"Only because it is fought by weak men."

"You judge yourself too harshly."

"You do not know what kind of man I am," said the prince, looking past her to the horizon.

"Then tell me."

He blinked, collecting his thoughts. "When my mind is not occupied I am beset by memories of the flights. The longing to soar again is a constant bewitchment on my life. My sleep is invaded by dreams of flying and nightmares that the webbed wings are my own. And sometimes the nightmare seems not horrible, but rather, my final peace. I would struggle no more. I would simply succumb and let myself become beast. That is what kind of man I am. So, my Lady, kindly be repulsed by me, for I find that less demeaning than pity."

"I have not pitied you, good sir," she countered.

"I saw it in your eyes when you tended my wound."

"You were mistaken. Neither do I find you repulsive. What other discourse is left to us?" said the princess seriously. But then she smiled engagingly at the prince and was glad to see a smile returned. The sparring match was ended, and the prince lowered his battle shield.

She was a woman who knew her mind. Their initial attraction did not prove wrong and within one year's time they were betrothed. Thoughts of the wedding night gave the prince new strength in resisting any flights. The longer he stayed away from the dragon, the more the scales softened. The ridge along his spine grew smaller. He longed to love his bride with as near the body of a man as possible. While traces of the scales would never wholly disappear— such was his fate—he was determined to reduce them as much as was within his power.

The wedding was celebrated by both kingdoms, and she came with the prince to live in his father's castle. For the first few months of marriage their happiness knew no bounds. Then, gradually, the princess sensed a discontent in her husband. There was a melancholy on his face, a distance sometimes in his eyes.

So she purposed to lavish more love on him. She instructed the cooks to prepare his favorite meals; she sewed royal tunics for him more fine than any ever seen in the kingdom. She wrote ballads about his bravery and strength set to wondrous melodies and sang them to him in front of his friends.

But each night he turned his back to her and fell asleep without a single caress. She wondered how she had failed him. Had some other maiden captured his heart away? So the princess braided her hair attractively with ribbons and flowers. She wore her finest gowns in his presence and perfumed her skin. She stayed by his side when they companied with others and gave him full attention whenever he spoke.

Finally, one night with tears in her eyes she asked him, "What is wrong? Why are you so far from me?"

"Nothing is amiss," he assured her. "I have never been happier. You imagine things because you are homesick. Go home for a time and visit your father."

"Perhaps you are right," she agreed, relieved at finding an answer.

But when she returned from the visit home, the prince was more aloof than ever. He moved away when she tried to embrace him in greeting. Something in his eyes reminded her of the shame and anger she had seen at their first encounter.

"My husband, surely something is wrong," she reached to embrace him again, but he grabbed her arms and held her away.

"Only just returned and already you are harping like a nursemaid," he chastised angrily. "I married to have a wife not a mother."

"Forgive me. Tell me what you want, and I will do it."

"Stop questioning me. Nothing is amiss except your incessant questioning."

That night when he fell asleep she curled quietly against his back to hold him without waking him. Something hard and knotted grew along his spine. She ran her hand beneath his nightshirt and pulled back in pain from the spiked and crusty scales that had grown there in her absence. At long last, she had her answer. He had fallen under the power of the dragon once again.

Now that she knew her enemy she could fight it. She would not let him meet the dragon tonight. Quietly, so as not to wake him, she pulled a sturdy sash from her wardrobe and tied his hands together. Then she bound the other end of the sash securely to the bedpost and waited.

When the moon rose yellow in the dark night he awoke and cursed upon discovering his tether.

"What is this?!" he demanded. "Are you mad, woman?"

"You don't have to go to the dragon," she said to comfort him. "I'll help you."

"You're a senseless woman. I arise to go to the privy."

"I'll bring you a chamber pot. I'll bring you anything you want. I love you."

"Then untie me," he demanded.

"I won't let you go."

He stared into her eyes momentarily, and the hatred there tore her heart. Then, without a word, he fumbled through his tunic that lay beside the bed and grasped a dagger with his tied hands. Quickly and easily he severed the sash and strode angrily from the room.

The next night she waited until he slept and then chained his hands to the bedpost. When he awoke he was enraged and kicked the post until it splintered apart from the headboard. She followed him from the room begging him to stay, but he left her behind.

Early the next morning she went to speak privately with his father. The Great King always took time for her, treating her as if she were one of his own daughters. She had enjoyed many walks with him here in the garden and marveled at the depth of his wisdom and kindness. They walked slowly. The King, with his hands clasped behind him, listened somberly as her concerns poured out like water. She finished and waited expectantly to hear his solution.

"Have you eaten today?" the King asked gently.

The princess was surprised by such a question. Whether or not she ate was of little import compared to saving the prince.

"I've had no appetite of late," she answered to be polite.

He reached into the branches of a fruit tree and handed her a ripe peach. "You must nourish yourself, my child."

She bit into the fruit only to please him and returned to the more pressing subject. "Will you send knights to restrain him or lock him in the dungeon?"

"Neither."

"What should we do?" she asked, perplexed.

"My son must make his own choices."

The princess could no longer contain herself. "You must do something before he is lost to us! You can't stand by and let him destroy himself. If you loved him as I do, you would stop him." Bitter tears wet her cheeks.

The King looked deep into her eyes. "Some wounds must be left open to heal."

That night when the prince rose to leave, the princess followed him from the bedroom clutching at the folds of his cloak. "I will do anything to keep from losing you. Take me with you on your dragon flights. I will become a beast with you."

"I would not love you if you were a beast," he yelled. "I would hate you as I hate myself. Flying is the only thing I love."

She clung desperately to his arm in the corridor, but he threw her against the stone wall and departed. So as not to wake any of the family in the nearby chambers, the princess choked back her sobs until she was once more in the privacy of her own rooms.

When two days passed and he did not return to the castle, the princess gathered others to search for him. Their calls rang out unanswered through wooded glens and mountain forests. After many days, only the princess continued searching. The others tried to dissuade her, but she paid no heed. No one, it seemed to her, could be counted on. The Great King least of all. He had not joined the search even once.

One day in the gnarled wood, her call into a cave was answered, but not by the prince. A leering troll lunged toward her from the darkness. Seemingly from nowhere, one of the King's knights appeared with raised sword and ran the wheezing creature off.

Recovering from her fright and turning her spooked horse toward the knight, the princess demanded, "How long have you been following me and who sent you? The King?"

"My Lady, by the King's command I have been following you since you began searching alone."

"Tell me," she said acidly, "why does the King concern himself with my safety when he refuses to protect his own son from the dragon? I would be in no danger if he had intervened on the prince's behalf a fortnight ago."

The knight had no answer to her query.

His duty soon ceased when winter fell and snow confined them to the castle. The princess grieved for her husband and feared he was dead or living out his days as a beast in some dark cave. She wept, remembering the laughter they had shared in their happiness and the tenderness in his strong embrace. Her heart had no songs to sing for months, and when she did finally pick up her lyre only songs of woe poured forth.

On her loom a tapestry took shape of dark and mournful colors. At times she lost herself in the weaving as she sorrowed; other times the loom sat for weeks untouched. Some days she unraveled whole sections of the tapestry with frustration over its mishappen state and nearly decided it was unsalvageable. She always gave her tapestries away as gifts, even though she dearly loved each one she created, but would never bestow such an unsightly thing as this on anyone.

If not for the icy roads she would have returned to her father's kingdom. She kept to herself and saw few people; she especially avoided the King. But, one morning she ventured from her chambers to watch the sunrise from the east tower and found the King standing there alone, as if he were waiting for her. She intended to turn away and leave without acknowledging him but found herself tolerating his presence instead.

They exchanged no words as the dawn, accompanied by rippled clouds of pink, played across the horizon. Then the princess's tears welled up beyond her control.

"All my life," the princess's words tumbled out between sobs, "I have brought healing to pain and solutions to problems. But when the person I most love needed me, I could not save him from harm."

The King put a comforting arm around her and spoke after she had quieted some. "There once was a kind-hearted woman who fed many people at her table. Young and old alike she lovingly waited on. So busy was she that she never took time to feed herself. And so eventually she collapsed from exhaustion and lack of nourishment. Then, finally, the woman took food and coming to her senses said, 'From now on I must eat when my guests eat.'"

When the princess returned to her chambers, she lifted her lyre intending to sing a lament, but instead a melancholy song about the sunrise took form. Later that week, she threaded bright colors in her loom to contrast with the deep rich tones of purple and blue already woven there. The strange colors and design that took shape brought an unexpected pleasure to her eyes and a peacefulness to her heart.

Outside, the first flowers were pushing up from the cold ground, and the soggy roads began to dry. Soon she would go home, although she knew she was welcome to stay. To celebrate the winter's thaw, a feast was held in the great hall. The aroma of roasted lamb filled the air as the princess, uneasy with the laughter and gaiety, held back at the fringe. But she desired to see her husband's brothers, sisters, and friends one last time before leaving. She thought it would feel strange to be among them without the prince at her side and was surprised to find it comfortable.

At first she ate of the banquet meal just to put her friends at ease since they all commented on her frailty. But, then, she began eating because the roasted lamb tasted wonderful. She drank refreshment because she was thirsty.

In the following weeks as the muddy roads dried, the princess completed the tapestry. It was like no other before it and, quite possibly, the most striking of all. Finally, it was fit to give to someone, but for the first time she considered keeping it for herself. "No," she debated within her heart, "that would be selfish. I shall give it to the Great King in thanks for his kindness."

On the day of her departure, she had the tapestry brought to the Great King during his morning walk in the garden. As the servants unfurled the weaving, the King smiled in appreciation of its unusual beauty.

"I cannot keep it. This tapestry must go with you," he said emphatically. "It is meant for your wall."

"I already have fine tapestries hanging in my chambers made by my mother and her sisters and my grandmother," she explained.

The King shook his head, "But they are not truly yours as this one is. Hang it where you can see and enjoy it daily."

He instructed the servants to place the tapestry in the coach that would take her home and then hugged the princess fondly in farewell.

○　　○　　○

Personal Reflection

Lady in Waiting

✍ Parts of the parable that touched me are . . .

✍ When I read these parts I felt . . .

✍ Similar situations in my life are . . .

Self-Nurturing: The princess had to let go of over-responsibility and, with the gentle encouragement of the Great King, she began to learn to nurture herself. Make a list of things you wish good friends would say to you and activities they would do with you.

Positive Messages

✍ _____

_____

_____

_____

_____

_____

Enjoyable Activities

✍ _____

_____

_____

_____

_____

_____

Be a best friend to yourself! Tell yourself the positive messages you wrote. Set aside some time for enjoyable activities, by yourself or with a friend.

Learning More: For more information about recovering from codependency, see Melody Beattie's books, *Codependent No More* and *Beyond Codependency.* Both are full of practical ways to nurture yourself and have healthy relationships.

DRAGON FLIGHT

○ ○ ○

The prince soared on the dragon's massive back and felt relieved now that he was no longer pulled between two worlds. Life was much easier now that he returned no more to his father's castle. It mattered not how beast-like he became. Flying from dusk to dawn and sleeping days in the dragon's warm winter lair, he did as he pleased without answering to anyone.

His legs grew bowed and bent. His face encrusted with scales until his nose became a snout with crooked and protruding sharp teeth. His back felt continually tight when he stood straight, so he hunched forward to be more comfortable.

Then one spring twilight, as he sailed the wind streams on the dragon, an incredible pain seized him. It was as if the flesh of his shoulders and back were rending asunder. The prince fell forward, grasping the dragon's neck lest he fall to his death during the convulsions. The dragon turned his head to appraise his charge and then smiled knowingly before whipping his neck to throw the prince off.

In shock and panic the prince fell through the air until, miraculously, wings opened around him. His fall turned into a swoop, and he alighted on the ground, stunned. The webbed wings folded neatly behind him. They were his own. Stretching them out on either side for inspection, the prince felt strangely satisfied. The metamorphosis was now complete. He no longer needed the dragon to fly; he was truly self-sufficient now.

Landing beside him, the dragon preened one of his own wings and purred, "You'll never be as large as I am, but this will make for some great fun in the air. Come on! Take off."

The prince flapped and wobbled into the sky. But his delight was short-lived, for the dragon swooped on him, slashing and clawing with glee.

"What are you doing?" cried the prince in angry disbelief as he dodged a taloned swipe.

"I am enjoying myself immensely," grinned the dragon. "Did you think carrying you around was all I wanted? I've been looking forward to this from the beginning."

The prince tried to escape an intentional downward slap of the dragon's wing, but it caught him. He careened through the air for some time before regaining control. A cat and mouse game of diving and chasing ensued until, exhausted and bleeding, the prince flew into the woods to hide.

Thereafter he tried to fly when the dragon was not in sight. However, as if with a sixth sense, the beast would appear and revel in his sadistic badgering. Even during the day, the dragon would quickly emerge from his lair whenever the prince ventured into the sky.

So it was that the prince found himself confined to the thickets of the wood. The need to fly would build inside him to an unbearable intensity, until once again he would risk an altercation with the dragon. After one such fleeting, unsatisfying moment in the sky, for which he paid dearly, the prince took refuge in the forest and sank into deep despair. The physical pain of his torn body and broken, trailing wing equalled the despondency of his soul. He slept fitfully and awoke with hunger pangs in addition to all his other woes. But, handicapped by his injuries, he could catch nothing to eat. The forest animals were all too fleet of foot for him now.

Then his ears heard a sound of jostling and clinking. He smelled a human approaching. Dragging himself to a vantage point above the forest road, he spied a tinker approaching who carried a huge pack of wares on his back. Here was prey slow enough to catch.

He maneuvered to a place of ambush and pounced, throwing the traveler to the ground. Perched on the tinker's stomach and snarling with anticipation of the kill, the prince lost heart when he saw the terror on the man's face. The thought of ripping into a human throat sickened him even though he had become accustomed to eating the raw flesh of animals. He threw the tinker aside and lurched back into the woods snorting and whimpering in misery.

It was then that he considered returning to his father's castle. He would be fed and sheltered there if the knights did not mistakenly kill him as he approached the battlements. Even that fate would be better than a slow death in the forest.

Half the day was already spent by the time he reached the edge of the woods and headed for the castle. He heard the watchmen call out an alarm as they spotted him and saw the knights positioning themselves on the road to do battle with the approaching threat. He stumbled weakly on, his broken wing dragging beside him.

The knights eyed him apprehensively and waited for the order to attack from their commander, an older brother of the prince.

"By the saints!" one knight exclaimed. "This dragon won't be much to dispatch. It's already half dead."

"And no bigger than a man at that," another added.

The prince fastened his eyes on the commander's and spoke hoarsely, "Help me, brother."

His brother's forehead furrowed, and urging his steed forward he guardedly approached the creature on the road. Abruptly he whirled his horse and called out to the knights, "Bring a litter to carry him into the castle. It is my younger brother returned."

The prince could not see clearly for a time because of the tears in his eyes, but as he wept he felt someone grasp his shoulder reassuringly. He folded himself onto the litter when it was brought and closed his eyes because he did not want to see the wincing faces of people in the courtyard. Women would gasp as he passed by. Children would run frightened to hide in the security of a mother's skirt. He opened his eyes fully only when the clunk of gates closing muffled the noise of onlookers and the sound of falling water told him he was in a private inner courtyard.

There his brothers washed his wounds in the wide fountain. His sisters brought a clean garment to cover him and carefully pulled his wings through slits they had cut in the cloth's back. He was relieved that his bride was not present and learned she had returned to her father's home long ago. In the privacy of his own chambers, he ate food brought for him until he was no longer hungry. When his father the King entered, the prince was again over-come with weeping so that he could not speak. Exhausted, he fell asleep with his father sitting beside the bed.

As the days passed the prince regained his strength and stayed closeted in his chambers lest he be a spectacle. He stood at his windows late at night when the courtyard below was empty of its normal bustle. The night air blowing on his face stirred the longing to fly once more. He flapped his broken wing to test its firmness and realized he could quietly glide to the courtyard floor undetected. The castle was asleep. He savored his short flight in the moonlight and then, feeling empty of soul, he climbed the stairs to his chambers once more. Despite the logs burning in the fireplace, his rooms seemed unusually dim, as if a dark cloud had obscured the moonlight. The prince recoiled when the darkness at the open window moved and one heavy, lidded eye of the dra-gon peered in at him from without. The beast hung like a great cockroach out-side upon the castle wall.

"Come out again," crooned the dragon in his low melodious voice. "I've missed your company."

"Do you think me a fool?" the prince answered.

"Perhaps I was too boisterous in our previous revelries," apologized the dragon. "I shall be more careful from now on."

"Be gone! I want nothing to do with you," the prince announced firmly in an effort to quell his rising desire to believe the dragon.

"Come," the creature purred deeply like a beckoning prostitute, and the prince stepped ambivalently toward the window. Perhaps it would be different this time. But, what if it wasn't? Yet, he would always wonder if he did not dare to find out.

Another voice spoke from behind him. "You know the truth."

The prince turned to see his father standing in the archway of the cham-ber door. Resentment welled up like bile into the prince's throat.

"The truth is I have had nothing to do with the dragon these many long days, yet I am as beastlike as ever. No scales have faded this time. Should I live out my days like this?" The prince extended his arms and wings for display.

"The scales will not fade until your wings are removed." His father's words brought a heaviness to the prince's heart.

From outside the window the dragon repositioned himself and exhaled a blast of fire in irritation. "Leave here! You are more kin to me than him now."

The prince turned back to his father. "If I cannot be human again, then let me go."

"If you do not wish to be whole again, then leave," said the King solemnly.

Once more the prince unfurled his webbed wings and then in anguish he bowed before his father. "Take your sword to them. Cut them off."

Snorting with disgust, the dragon launched noisily into the night air, and his departure sent chilly gusts through the window.

"Sever them quickly," the prince begged, "before I lose my resolve."

"They cannot be severed," the King explained gravely. "They must be pulled out."

"Do whatever you must."

"Stand and hold tightly to me," said the King as he put his arms around his son. With both hands, the King firmly grasped the base of one wing. His strong hands pulled steadily, and the prince's shoulder felt ablaze. As the sinews of the wing tore from the muscles in his back, a beastly wail escaped the prince's lips. Though nearly unconscious from the searing pain, the prince felt his father's hands grasp the remaining wing.

"No!" He wrenched away, falling against the wall. On the floor beside him, in the flickering firelight from the hearth, lay the first wing. From the flesh of its bloodied base long tendrils of sinew curled and writhed like newly unearthed worms. The prince gasped in revulsion at what had been hosted in his body. "Take the other one," he whispered, and though unable to stand he wrapped his arms around his father's waist.

Over the long days, as the gaping wounds in his back healed, the prince was attended by his brothers and sisters. Some of them had ridden the dragon in the past. Some confessed to him that they still struggled, but were strengthened in their abstinence by seeing the prince's fate.

When he was able to sit up he asked for parchment and ink to write his bride. On his sickbed he had tossed and turned with regret for his churlish treatment of her. He did not ask her to return or even to forgive him, but wrote only to list his many offenses against her and to tell her of his remorse. Although he felt great sadness, sending the letter brought a melancholy peace to his soul. There were others to make amends to, but no one else he had mistreated as miserably as his wife. He could now see clearly how he had punished her for his own weaknesses.

One summer day a sister entered his chambers bursting with excitement. "Your wife has come to the castle!" she exclaimed, expecting him to be gladdened. But the prince was dismayed.

"I don't want to see her," the prince said with dread. "Not after all that has happened. I cannot see her . . ."

"But she is *here.*" Biting her lip, the sister gestured toward the entrance to his rooms. His wife stood silently in the doorway with a strange mixture of emotions on her face.

The prince instantly turned away as if to hide his appearance. He heard the sister excuse herself to leave them alone and then his wife's voice.

"I will not batter at your heart to gain entrance as I did before. If you wish me to leave, I will do so."

He turned, so that she could not see him fully, but just from the side. "Good Lady, please stay," he requested and found her coming near to him. She reached out and placed a soft hand on his reptilian cheek. He could barely feel her touch through the thick, scaled skin.

"How can you stand to look at me, let alone touch me?" He dared to look into her eyes.

"My husband, do not bother yourself with such vanity. You were never overly handsome to begin with." She tried to hide a smile as she spoke, but let it loose when a chuckle escaped from the prince in spite of himself. Laughter broke forth from his snout like piglet snorts, and he silenced himself abruptly in embarrassment.

"I am undeserving of any attention from you."

"That may be, but let us not repeat our previous patterns of you feeling ashamed and of me trying desperately to dislodge you from it. We have had enough of shame and guilt. They are ponderous garments I no longer wear, and garments I do not desire to see you wear. Let us both cast them aside for new clothes."

"I fear our habits will not be that easily replaced," the prince said with misgiving.

"No doubt we shall both have to work at it," she agreed.

The snout flattened slowly. With the passage of years the scales softened and faded until only faint traces were visible. There were, indeed, times of temptation for the prince, but never again did he ride the dragon.

He could easily detect when others were ensnared, as in the case of a younger brother who looked as if he were off to hunt with his falcon. But, the prince could tell his true intent. He recognized the hunger in his brother's eyes; he knew too well the innocent pretense on the younger man's face. It was a pretense the prince had conjured often himself.

"Don't go, brother," said the prince.

"What are you talking about? Perfect day for a hunt," smiled the brother as he cinched the livery on his horse.

"We both know it is the dragon you intend to find."

"What if I do?" The younger man was suddenly surly.

"Remember what happened to me."

"I won't let it go that far." The brother climbed onto his horse and reached for the waiting falcon on its perch.

"The change comes quickly for some without any warning."

"No," the brother disagreed. "I don't spend enough time with the dragon for that to happen. There's no harm in a good ride every now and then. I make the dragon *my* slave," he laughed confidently and kicked his steed into a canter.

The prince watched him go and sadly shook his head, hoping his brother would see the truth soon.

o   o   o

P e r s o n a l   R e f l e c t i o n

Dragon Flight

✍ Parts of the parable that touched me are . . .

✍ When I read these parts I felt . . .

✍ Similar situations in my life are . . .

Becoming a dragon was painful and disappointing for the prince. The final stages of self-defeating behavior are never as exciting as the early experiences. The pain far outweighs the initial pleasure as the behavior progresses. Make a list of the initial attractions of your dragon and the reality as your dragon took over.

Flying with the dragon

Initial attractions were . . . _____
_____
_____
_____
_____
_____

Actual experiences when the dragon turned on me . . .
_____
_____
_____
_____
_____
_____

Hitting bottom! _____
_____
_____
_____
_____
_____

If you were going to attend a support group someday, which of those listed in Resources, page 177, would you choose? As a next step, call the 800 number or look up the local number and find out about meetings in your area. If you feel hesitant, don't decide now whether or not you will attend. Your goal at this moment is just to get information about the time and location of the meeting.

Group name: _____

Day and Time: _____

Location and directions: _____

_____

CASTLE SAFE I

○   ○   ○

A *fair and gentle princess lived alone in a castle with the only gate* barred securely from within and the drawbridge closed tightly against the battlements.

The castle was once full of relatives, vassals, serfs, and guests, but the princess had banished every last one of them. When she locked them out, she vowed never again to let people come and go freely in her castle.

She wept as she toiled and thought of the many years of diligence she would need to repair the wreckage that had been made of her home. Gardens had been trodden down by careless feet. Tapestries had been torn from the walls and soiled in drunken revelries. Other cherished articles were missing altogether, having been stolen by those she once trusted.

"How could you be so foolish as to think that any of them ever cared about you?" she angrily chastised herself as she worked.

Now and then marauders crossed the moat, hoping to scale the battlements with their ropes, but the great walls were far too high for the success of any such attempt. The princess lived safe in her fortress with only a scullery cat for companionship.

Each day she thankfully drank in the solitude as she labored to restore her sanctuary. Sunlight slowly played across the courtyard until shadows came and the air carried the smoky smell of meals cooking in hearths of the nearby village. Then the princess finished her tasks for the day and stoked her own fire to prepare soup for herself and the gray brindle cat.

Like most cats, he carried himself as though he were master of the castle and tolerated such indignities as being held or caressed. Unlike others of his kind, he relished the bread and hot vegetables that the princess put in his bowl. He would watch attentively until the vessel was filled, then he carried it off in his mouth to eat somewhere in regal privacy.

As twilight hastened to evening, the princess, with taper in hand to light her way, wearily climbed the narrow stone stairway to her bedchambers. When the wind came from the east at night, it sounded like a mournful wail blowing against the unmoving walls and empty towers of the castle.

So the days and nights passed until one evening at mealtime the princess, for amusement, decided to follow the cat and see where he preferred to banquet. Would he sit in a window casement overlooking the darkening valley? Perhaps he fancied the war hall where armor and lances lined the walls. But, no he disappeared instead into the downward spiral leading to the dungeons.

"I shall not follow you there," the princess said with distaste. "No doubt you hunt vermin below."

"I wonder," she asked herself, "if he actually eats the vegetables and bread or only uses them for bait to catch rodents. I might as well give him stale fare if that is so." So the next night at supper, the princess followed him once again, this time with a taper to light the dungeon stairway.

The damp, musty air of the dungeon crept into her nostrils even before the stairwell widened into the underground expanse. She heard a rustle and a scampering in the scattered patches of straw on the uneven bedrock floor. Wrinkling her nose in disgust at the thought of the disreputable creatures scurrying from the flickering light, the princess gathered her skirts with her free hand before continuing. Iron bars of a cell to her left cast shifting double shadows, and the princess caught a glimpse of the brindle cat there. Moving closer, she spied a larger shape beside the cat. The princess gasped when the candlelight revealed human eyes staring back at her. It was a child, as terrified as the princess, fearfully clutching the cat to her breast as if to ward off some evil.

"How did you get in here?" the princess demanded angrily. The child cringed but did not speak. "Answer me!" It was an imperial decree.

"Someone locked me in when you banished everyone," the child sobbed.

Incredulous, the princess walked closer to the bars of the cell. "How could that be? What have you eaten these many long days?"

"Sir Thom brought me food," said the child, hugging the cat tighter. The animal squirmed to regain some degree of propriety and then jumped free to sit a safe distance from any human reach. The child was a disheveled and dirty sight, hair matted and uncombed, clothes tattered and filthy. While relieved that the child had not entered by some secret passage, the princess was never-theless not pleased to have a guest.

"Come," the princess commanded, taking a key from the wall. "I shall put you out of here and out of the castle."

"No," cried the child. "Not out of the castle!"

"You can go to the village—it's close by—and find your parents."

"I have no parents. I've always lived in the castle. Please don't put me out," the child begged with a wail that echoed loudly in the dungeon.

"Hush that noise!" Sorely irritated, the princess waited impatiently by the open rusty door. "Come out. *Now!*"

She was answered only by a whimper and watched the child retreat fur-ther into the cell. Using force would require touching the child's lice-ridden body, and the princess wanted nothing to do with that.

"I can see we are at odds on this." She tried to be calm. "Very well then. I won't put you out of the castle tonight. So come out of the cell."

The child responded to the kinder voice and came hesitantly forward. Upstairs, the little girl took a warm bath in a round copper pan by the hearth while the princess searched in old trunks for clothes she wore as a child. The muslin nightshirt hung loosely on the little girl's bony frame. She was given a hearty meal and then put to bed. The princess fully intended to put the child out the next day.

In the morning she awoke to the sound of whimsical giggling. Going to her window, she saw the child dancing in the sunlit courtyard and warbling an endless sing-song tune.

"What are you doing?" the princess asked austerely.

"I like the sunshine," came the sheepish reply from the suddenly subdued child.

"Come inside. It's time to breakfast."

"Yes, my Lady."

Sir Thom joined them at the hearth but showed no interest in the bread laid down for him.

"Don't worry," the child offered comfort, noting the concerned face of the princess. "He eats lots of mice in the dungeon, except for their feet and tails. Those probably taste like gristle."

"Do not speak of such things while I eat," commanded the princess.

The quiet lasted only a short while before the child began humming between and during mouthfuls of porridge. A reprimanding glance from the princess silenced that. Some moments later the child broke the solitude again.

"I was very lonely in the dungeon. Don't you get lonely?"

"No."

"Why not?"

"I have many things to do. Today I will sweep out the east chambers."

"May I help?" The child moved eagerly to the edge of her seat.

"I suppose," agreed the princess, thinking she could always put the child out tomorrow. So they labored together in the east chambers, and the small girl commented on how terrible it was that people had made such an awful mess and no wonder the princess banished them all. Then as she worked, the child chanted silly rhymes to entertain herself. The princess almost smiled a time or two from what she overheard.

With the day's work done and the evening meal finished, the princess sat by the hearth in the great hall watching the child cuddle Sir Thom and sing songs to him. Sprawled on her lap, the cat now and then batted a paw at the child's tangled locks of hair.

"Let me braid your hair." The princess found herself saying, and the child's face brightened with delight. The princess brushed out the tangles gently, for she remembered the yanks her nursemaid had inflicted on her. Then she wove a long braid starting from the top of the child's head. When it was done the child danced elegantly around the hall. For her, every simple pleasure was an occasion for celebration.

The princess had forgotten how good it felt to laugh. Still, she intended to put the child out tomorrow.

The next day the princess was hard at work early scrubbing the floors in the east wing. The child hopped and jumped in the doorway where the princess had warned her to stay as she mopped.

"Let me help. What can I do to help?" pestered the child. So the princess sent her to fetch a clean bucket of water. When she did not return in a timely fashion, the princess went searching for her.

In the courtyard, she found her young charge straining at the wooden wheel that raised the iron gate and lowered the drawbridge.

"What do you think you're doing?"

"On my way to the well I heard someone calling to be let in."

"Foolish child! You must never, *ever* open this gate to anyone."

"But he said he's a vassal of yours." The child was in tears from the furious reprimand.

Climbing swiftly into the tower above the gate, the princess peered down through the narrow window high above the visitor. "Be gone from here or I shall pour boiling oil upon your head!" she announced. Hearing such a threat, the caller speedily reigned his horse around and departed.

"To think you would have given him entrance," the princess chastised the child who had followed her into the tower. "He was one of the worst of the sots I banished. He will never set foot in this castle again as long as I live. Whatever possessed me? I was actually considering letting you stay before this."

"I didn't know he was a bad person. Please don't be angry with me," sobbed the child, who wrapped her tiny arms desperately around the princess's legs. "Please let me stay here with you. I promise I'll be good."

The princess was irritated to feel her anger melting. "Stop that," she said in discomfort as she gently pried the child off and then brushed her skirt to compose herself. The little girl stood beside her, snuffling and looking up with wide eyes.

"If you wish to stay here you must promise never to open this gate to anyone," offered the princess reluctantly.

Nodding solemnly, the child sealed the agreement.

○   ○   ○

Personal Reflection

Castle Safe I

✍ Parts of the parable that touched me are . . .

✍ When I read these parts I felt . . .

✍ Similar situations in my life are . . .

<u>*The Child in Me:*</u> We all have an inner child. It is the part of us that carries the memories of our growing up years. It is a part of us that plays and has fun. Many adults in recovery find that they (or someone else) locked away the inner child long ago. To live a balanced life, we must reclaim our past and get to know ourselves again.

In the space below, write yourself two letters, one from the point of view of the child you were and one from your adult point of view.

Using your non-dominant hand, write a letter from you the child to you the adult. Where has this inner child been kept? What does this part need from you to feel safe and nurtured? What does the inner child enjoy doing for fun? Does she/he have a nickname or favorite name? How old is your inner child?

Dear _____,

_____

_____

_____

_____

_____

_____

_____

_____

_____

_____

_____

_____

_____

_____

_____

Now, with your dominant hand, write a reply to your child self from your adult self. What do you like about your inner child? What qualities of this child self are you uncomfortable with? How would you like to nurture your inner child better? (This might include setting loving limits on out-of-control behavior.) How can you play more?

Dear _____,

Go ahead, have some fun! Buy some modeling clay, some finger paints, bubbles, a ball, whatever appeals to you. Spending some time playing is a wonderful way to let your child out of the dungeon.

○ ○ ○

*T*he princess found herself irritated sometimes at the child, but more often she enjoyed the silly chatter and spontaneous antics of her young friend. She wondered at how such a small person, who wiggled and skipped all day, could have so much energy even into the night.

"Tell me another story," begged the little girl from her bed.

"Two is enough. Go to sleep now."

"I like the ones about handsome princes who rescue princesses from monster dragons. Do you hope a handsome prince will come to rescue you?"

"No. Go to sleep now," said the princess pulling her own bedcovers up around her.

"Has a handsome prince ever come here for you?"

"Once." The princess remembered with distaste. "He camped outside the walls for weeks vowing he would not return home without me as his bride. Every day I would hear him calling out trying to convince me of his love."

"Was he handsome and kind?" asked the child excitedly.

"So they all seem at first. But most likely he had heard of some castle filled with treasure and wished to make it his own. I stayed away from the windows and never spoke to him. Finally, he gave up his vigil."

"But how would you know whether he was good hearted or evil unless you spoke with him?"

"No one is truly good hearted."

"How can that be?" The child was perplexed.

"Those who are evil do their damage. Those who seem good hearted stand by and do nothing. If you are wise, you will trust no one."

Eyebrows pulled together, the child pondered these things. "I don't know how to recognize the bad people. You don't know how to recognize those who are good. Surely there must be some way to do both."

"I think not."

"The Great King could tell us," mused the child aloud. "He knows everything wise and good."

"But his city is far away and we have no way to ask him," said the princess tiredly. "Now go to sleep."

The next day was filled with sunlight and crisp gusty wind.

"Come play hide and seek with me in the courtyard!" said the child, pulling insistently at the princess's skirt.

"I am busy now. Bother me not. If you had your way, nothing would get done and all would be play."

"Just for a short while, come outside," begged the child.

"Very well. But then you must help with the work."

So it was that as they laughed in the garden, the voices of someone at the gate came to them on the wind. It was a daughter of the Great King accompanied by two of her brothers. Climbing into the tower, the princess could see them clearly.

"Dear friend," called the daughter of the Great King upon spying her at the narrow window, "we heard your castle had been pillaged and have come to your aid. How happy we are to see you alive. Are you well?"

"Yes, I am well. Please return home and do not concern yourselves further. Forgive me for not extending to you the kind hospitality that I received so often in past visits to your home, but I open the gates to no one anymore."

"We bring wood and canvas and weaving flax, for we hear that much needs to be repaired. Have you need of these things?"

"Yes, but I cannot let you enter."

"Then we shall leave the goods here for you, and when we depart you can bring them in. Tell me what else you have need of, and I shall bring it on my next visit."

"You are too gracious, friend. Do not bother yourselves any further on my account. Be safe on your journey home." With that the princess left the window while the child, barely tall enough to see out, strained for a last glimpse of the departing visitors.

"It would be such fun to invite guests in," the child said wistfully. "I would give them flowers."

"They would probably crush them."

"I would ask for a drink from their traveling flasks."

"It would, most likely, be bitter," warned the princess.

"We would sing songs together."

"They would, in all likelihood, sing their songs, but not yours."

"How do you know it would be so disappointing? Has any harm ever come to you by them?" the child persisted, following the princess down the tower's circular stairway to the courtyard.

"No, but all people are alike."

"Couldn't we ask them in, just this once and find out if they're different?

"No."

"Next time they come?" the child asked with a last bit of hope.

"They won't return after such a dour reception," the princess replied.

But she was mistaken, for when the winter thawed, they came once again with wood, canvas, and flax for weaving.

Again the princess spoke to them from the tower window. "I am touched by your kindness. Please do not think me ungrateful, but I cannot let you in." Meanwhile, the child, with her nose at the stone sill, made a wild toss of something out the narrow window. A flower fell into the lap of the Great King's daughter, and she smiled warmly. After lifting the blossom to her face to enjoy the fragrance, she tucked the flower happily into the braid crowning her head.

"See there! She didn't crush it! Can't we invite her in?" the child asked expectantly despite the struggle on the face of the princess.

"Very well, but only into the courtyard. And her brothers must stay outside."

So the drawbridge was lowered and the gate raised for the first time since the banishment, though not without misgiving on the princess's part. No sooner had their visitor entered than the heavy iron gate was protectively lowered once more.

"What have you carried to drink on your journey?" asked the child, bouncing beside the calm horse as the guest dismounted.

"Water from a fresh spring." The King's daughter graciously handed the excited child the goatskin flask.

Holding it over her head, the child let water splash on her face and drop into her mouth. "It's not bitter," she exclaimed dancing and held the flask out to the apprehensive princess.

The three walked in the garden talking and enjoying the flowers that were budding.

"I know a song about a bird," said the child before launching into the tune. The King's daughter joined in, harmonizing with her, and then taught her a new verse.

"You're a lot nicer than we thought you'd be," exclaimed the child as the princess smiled in embarrassment. But the King's daughter laughed good-naturedly.

Many times the Great King's daughter came to see the princess and sat in the garden with her. Not one stalk was broken; no plants were trampled by the guest. So, eventually the princess even invited her friend into the hall to show her how the restoration continued.

Many were the visits they enjoyed while the brothers waited patiently outside the walls. Then, one day, the child threw flowers out the window to them as the princess turned the wooden wheel to open the gate for the King's daughter to enter.

"Look! They didn't crush the flowers either!" cried the child tugging at the princess's skirt and pointing toward the young men.

"I don't care. They are not coming in here," insisted the princess.

"But, they must get tired waiting for their sister outside all the time. They come all this way to protect her on her journey. Surely they would do you no harm. Can't we just let them into the courtyard where they can rest under the shade of the trees?"

"There are trees outside where they can lounge."

The child huffed in exasperation, "But we can't sing songs with them out there."

"My brothers do like to sing," commented the King's daughter leading her horse across the drawbridge.

"Please," begged the child. "Just this once. If they do anything unseemly, you can always banish them. But, if you don't invite them in, you'll never find out for yourself if they are good hearted. And it's not like they are total strangers. You already know lots about them from the King's daughter."

Biting her lower lip in consternation, the princess eyed the young men as they smiled at her. "Maybe just this once. But only into the courtyard."

Not only did they sing that afternoon, but one brother also told stories of battles with dragons and trolls the likes of which the child had never heard. The other brother played his lute so lively that even the princess tapped her feet.

When they left with their sister, the child waved good-bye humming a new tune she had just learned. "Aren't you glad you let them in?" she asked the princess.

"I suppose they were pleasant enough."

"And ever so handsome," giggled the little girl.

"I didn't notice," lied the princess wondering what it might be like to invite them into her hall someday.

True to her vow, and rightly so, people never again came and went *freely* from the castle. The gate remained closed and the drawbridge drawn up except for the most select of guests who did not crush flowers thrown to them. Those who carried no bitter drink were allowed into the gardens where they sang songs with the princess and the child. Of those guests, only the most trustworthy were invited into the hall and inner rooms of her castle.

So it was that the gentle princess and little child remained safe, but no longer alone.

○　　　○　　　○

Personal Reflection

Castle Safe II

✍ Parts of the parable that touched me are . . .

✍ When I read these parts I felt . . .

✍ Similar situations in my life are . . .

Outside the Walls
I've banished . . . ☞ _____

(List specific people _____
and categories of people, _____
for example, _____
all women or men, _____
all people who _____
remind me of someone, _____
and so on.) _____
These people are _____
not safe because . . . _____

Hall and Inner Rooms
I let these close friends in . . .
I decided they were trustworthy because . . .

_____
_____
_____
_____

Where is your Higher Power in this picture? What has God done to be trustworthy? Or what must God do to win your trust?

Do you want to shift some hurtful people to a less close level of intimacy? Even banish some?

Have some people who might be potential friends been unfairly locked outside the gate?

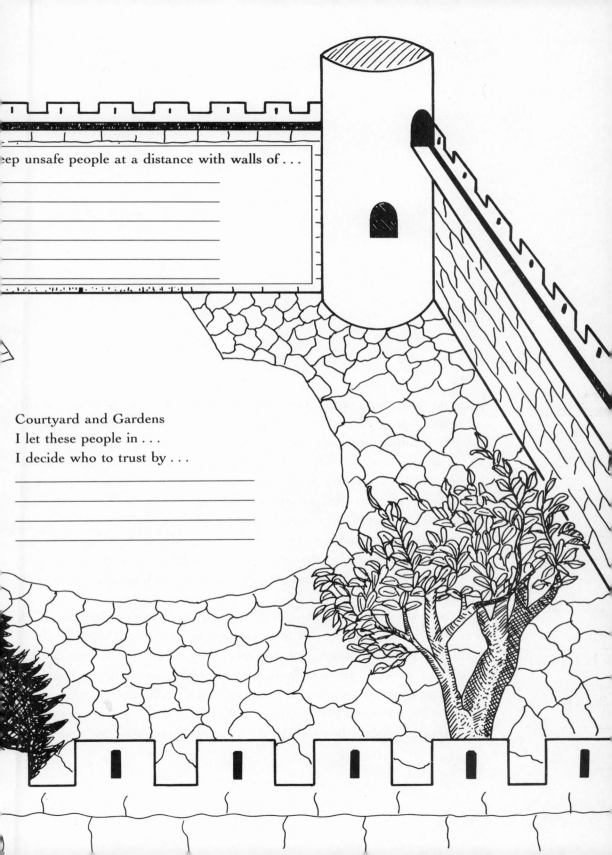

...eep unsafe people at a distance with walls of . . .

_____
_____
_____
_____
_____

Courtyard and Gardens
I let these people in . . .
I decide who to trust by . . .

_____
_____
_____
_____

MIRROR, MIRROR

o   o   o

She was born into a dark and war-torn land, the youngest child and only daughter of the king and queen. Because of the battles, her father and older brothers spent little time in the castle.

At the outset of the wars, they had thought themselves sure to defeat the sorcerer and his army. But one by one, over the years, allies in neighboring kingdoms fell until this one land was left standing alone, a small and withering enclave in the midst of the sorcerer's conquered domains.

One last hope remained. There were rumors of a Great King far to the north with might far greater than the sorcerer's. When the princess was nearly fifteen, envoys were sent to plead for help. The besieged kingdom waited with heavy hearts.

Would the disguised envoys find safe passage through enemy occupied lands? Why should this Great King release knights to their aid when they had no alliance? For that matter, did the Great King really exist, or was he the fabricated hope of all those suffering under the conqueror's oppression?

The sorcerer's dark power kept the sky continually overcast, shrouding all with chill and dread. No radiant sunlight had warmed the land for years. The nights were black because the thick clouds smothered any moonlight.

In the cover of this darkness one night, a band of misshapen gnomes climbed silently from the depths beneath the castle cisterns and crept unseen into the chambers of the sleeping princess. She awoke with a start to find small bodies like rats clamoring onto her bed. Though she opened her mouth to scream, only the whisper of a cry escaped and her body seemed frozen in terror.

"Gnome got your tongue?" teased one of the intruders, and the rest cackled and wriggled gleefully around her. "You can't betray us, because you're one of us, a changeling we switched with the real princess in infancy. So, be thankful to us for your lofty state and remember whence you came!"

"Look how big my little girl has grown," wheezed one leering hag. "We boiled the real baby princess and gave you the broth to make you human sized, but you're still one of us."

Finding her voice and strength at last, the princess screamed aloud and leaped from her bed to run for her mother's room. Guards were sent at once to the princess's chambers, but they found no trace of any intruders.

"You've had a nightmare, that is all," the queen reassured her daughter and held her close.

The next morning, the princess went to her mirror as usual to brush her hair and noticed for the first time how bulbous her nose was. Indeed, the longer she looked the more she realized that it was quite unsightly, large and pug, like a pig's. And her eyes! How beady they were, set deep above her wide cheekbones. She fell to the floor crying in anguish, for she knew then that her midnight visitors were no dream and that their words were true. All that day she stayed in her room weeping and would see no one. At eventide she fell asleep, heartsick and exhausted, only to be awakened once more by the grotesque band of wriggling gnomes.

"You're one of us!" they sang hoarsely, dancing about her chambers wildly. "Call the guards on us once more, and we'll tell your heritage to all the castle!" Pilfering through her belongings, they wreaked havoc in the room until dawn, when they crept back to their underground abode, taking whatever they fancied. The smell of their putrid little bodies lingered in the room long after their departure. Each night the princess suffered their harassment, and during the days she kept to herself, eating little of the food concerned servants brought. The raucous gnomes during their nightly visitations bandied the leftovers about. Tossing the food among themselves as they belched and ate, the gnomes had a great feast.

Then they regularly brought out the mirror, which the princess had hidden because she could not bear to look at herself. Pulling the reluctant princess to stand before it, they reveled in pointing out every gnomelike aspect of her features.

"Stop, stop!" she cried, covering her face with her hands. "Stop, stop," they mimicked her plea with relish, for they knew what the princess did not: The image she saw was untrue. On their first visit, before awakening the princess, the gnomes had enchanted her mirror to reflect a horrible visage so that she would believe their terrible lies.

On her fifteenth birthday there was to be a banquet and celebration held in her honor. Although the princess begged her mother to cancel the festivities, the queen would not hear of it.

"You have been ill in your room too long, my child," said the queen. "A celebration in these bleak times will do us all good."

"How can you be so cruel to me?" the princess protested angrily.

"What are you talking about?" the queen asked in disbelief.

"It is unbearable to move among people and know that they either pity me or make light of me out of hearing."

"Why would anyone pity or make light of you?"

"Because I am ugly!"

"Nonsense," said the queen, cupping the princess's face in her hands. "You are beautiful."

In that moment, the princess decided that the queen must be blinded by misplaced maternal love. While thankful for her devotion, the daughter nonetheless thought the woman a kind-hearted fool. "She would not look on me so graciously if she knew the truth of my parentage," grieved the princess.

At the birthday celebration, the princess wore her hair long and hanging down on either side to cover her face as much as possible. Keeping her chin tucked, she peered out from under her locks only when necessary and avoided the humiliation of meeting anyone's eyes. She had no desire to see the false kindness there, the manufactured pleasantness extended only because of her royal station.

While her father could not leave the battle lines, two of her brothers came home for a rest along with a handful of other weary knights. A strained mirth filled the banquet hall, as if all attending wondered whether it would be their last gathering. But the playing of lutes and horns encouraged the guests to dance in a circle with hands linked in the air.

"Lovely Lady?" a friend of her brother inquired, inviting her to dance with him. She had long thought him the kindest and most handsome knight ever, but now was cut to the quick by his callous treatment. How dare he mock her before the people! She felt her face redden with shame at the imagined snickers that his charity would elicit from the guests.

"No," she mumbled and drew back, staring at the floor until she saw his feet leave. Another pair of boots approached.

"Dance with me, Princess," the man bellowed gregariously. She recognized the voice at once. It belonged to the belligerent son of one of her father's dukes. She had always avoided his uncomely advances.

"No," she mumbled once again, but he grabbed her hand and dragged her into the circle. When the dance was over he stayed by her side and, for once, she was thankful for his incessant boasting, mostly about his supposed feats in battle. For when anyone joined them, she was protected from conversation.

After some time, her brother pulled her aside. "Why are you encouraging him, little sister?"

"And why shouldn't I?" she replied testily.

"Because he is a dolt."

"I'm fifteen now. I shall choose my own suitors, thank you." With that she returned to the loud knight and placed her hand in the crook of his arm.

Suddenly a herald from the front lines burst into the room, his clothes spattered with mud from his hasty journey. Worry lining her face, the queen rose slowly from the royal dais overlooking the hall.

"My Queen, Lords and Ladies." The messenger bowed low before the dais. "We have heard news. A great army is moving in the north against the sorcerer!"

In the crowd, a murmur of shocked disbelief became a joyful cheer.

Over the following months, news came to them of the advancing army's victories. Was it the Great King? All they knew was that the attacking forces were readily routing the sorcerer's troops and might reach their city before the year's end. While the sky over their land remained overcast, the clouds began to separate. Here and there, for the first time in years, the sun broke through in glorious shafts of light. Alone in her chambers, the princess watched the display in awe. Before her eyes, a sunbeam glided through her window and struck the cast-aside mirror. Dust floating in the beam sparkled gold and silver as the princess reached out to pass her hand through the gossamer light.

As she moved, the princess caught a glimpse of herself in the mirror and gasped. The face was no longer that of a gnome but the contours of her own true appearance, both familiar and new at the same time. Happy tears and laughter broke forth from the face she watched in the mirror. Unable to contain herself, she danced joyfully in the light of the sunbeam.

"It was enchanted!" she shouted. "The gnomes must have bewitched my mirror, but now I know the truth! Everything they said was a lie!"

She swept her hair upward and secured the tresses with ivory combs. Then she sent word to the loud son of the duke, excusing herself from a riding engagement previously made. "No more of him," she announced to herself.

That night she intentionally suffered the grotesque visitation of the gnomes without a word about her discovery. Then as dawn and their departure neared, she begged them to leave, knowing full well by now that, just to vex her, they always did the opposite of any request.

"Leave? Leave! You want *us* to leave!" badgered one disheveled gnome, who fanned the others into frenzied rollicking.

"Stay away from me," she pleaded purposefully, as she backed toward the shuttered windows that had closed out the night air. The gnomes rudely crowded around her, hissing and sneering. Turning as if to hide her face against the shutters, the princess peered through a crack in the wood to see the rim of the rising sun not yet enveloped by the waiting canopy of broken clouds. Her quick hands threw open the shutters, and she stood back to let the sunlight flood her motley guests.

With unholy shrieks, they fell to the stone floor in convulsions and withered like so many pieces of dried fruit. She put her hands to her ears to shut out the last of the tormented cries, for, despite all their wickedness, she regretted causing them pain. The shrunken bodies, reduced to dry papery wisps, were caught up in a gust of wind like autumn leaves. They whirled into the air and began to sparkle in the sunlight. To the amazement of the princess, they suddenly blossomed into delicate fairies with translucent wings. Laughing and crying with joy, they sounded like the chiming of tiny crystal bells.

"Thank you! Thank you!" one cried out, floating on the morning breeze. "You've freed us from the sorcerer's spell. Forgive us, Princess. In our accursed state, we spread our misery to all we found. We were, to you, most unkind of all. Forgive us, for we, too, had forgotten our true nature."

As the breeze stirred again, they glided through the open window. The soft wind fluffed the princess's hair gently, and with happy wonderment, she watched the fairies fly away.

○   ○   ○

Personal Reflection

Mirror, Mirror

✍ Parts of the parable that touched me are . . .

✍ When I read these parts I felt . . .

✍ Similar situations in my life are . . .

<u>*Self-Reflection: How do I see myself?:*</u> Use the three mirrors below to get a clearer picture of who you are. Jot down whatever comes quickly to mind. Use words or short phrases to describe your intelligence, skills, personality, physical appearance.

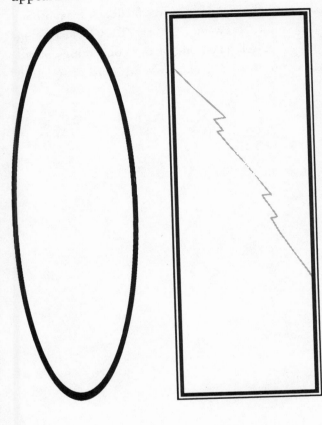

How I See Myself
Positives and
Negatives

How Critical People
See Me

How Positive People
See Me

Is my view of myself closer to: (check one)
The critical mirror ☐   The positive mirror ☐
A mix of both ☐

Critical Mirror: Is anything here an actual character defect that you need to work on? (Mark an "x" by them.)

What is unfounded or unfair in this mirror? Draw a line through them.

Positive Mirror: A poor self-concept will discount positive feedback from others with thoughts such as, "If they really knew me . . ." or "They're just being nice, but don't really mean it . . ." Circle each one of the good things about you in your positive mirror. As you do so, say each one out loud completing the sentence, "I'm so glad I'm . . ."

THE PAINTING

o   o   o

The painting was exquisite. Though not even half finished, the painter could see it would be uniquely beautiful. This was truly a work fit to hang in the hall of the Great King.

The painter stood back from the canvas, brush in hand, and surmised his work. He was eager to continue, but the late afternoon light streaming in the castle windows was not the best to paint in. So he set about cleaning his brushes. Tomorrow morning he would continue. Then the room would be filled with fresh light from the wide balcony windows.

As he removed his apron, his eyes wandered lovingly over the gentle, rolling hills of the painted landscape. The colors, the shadows, the textures were harmonious and peaceful: the azure sky, the deep teals of the lake, and the emerald green of the hills. Tomorrow he would give life to the distant mountains by carefully swathing them in purples.

When he returned the next morning to paint, he was greeted by a sight too horrible to believe. The easel was knocked over and the canvas had fallen onto the floor. Hideous blotches of something black marred his landscape.

"No!" the painter cried out in anguish, holding the canvas in his outstretched arms. Who would have done such a cruel and senseless deed? What reason could anyone have for such destruction? The painter had no enemies in the castle of the Great King. Only friends and loved ones abode here.

"Why?" he called out, releasing the rage in his soul. He tried to wipe off the blotches, but they were thick and set like dried tar. The sharpest knife did not scrape the material off. Neither was it possible to cover over it; the paint only beaded up on the layered, slick black surface. It was then that he despaired, for he realized there was no way to salvage the painting. It was hopelessly marred.

Looking at the wretched canvas was too painful to bear. The idyllic hillsides and calm lake gasped for life where they emerged from the blotches. The pure blue of the sky was a pathetic reminder now of what the painting could have been. He hated the very sight of it. A mockery of promise. A ludicrous monstrosity.

In blind pain he slashed the canvas with dark paint from his own brush. There. It was thoroughly ruined now and, at least, in harmony with itself once again.

The painter sat before the canvas weeping with his head in his hands for the rest of the day. When evening fell he heard the sound of someone shuffling toward him in the room, but he was too exhausted to raise his head.

"What do you want?" he asked scathingly. "Leave me alone!"

"Such a shame," said the person hoarsely. "There's no reason to paint any longer. You might as well throw yourself out the window."

The painter was surprised that someone actually understood the depth of the wound to his soul. Looking up, he visually searched the darkened room, but found no one. Then turning toward the balcony, his eyes fell on the scabrous outline of a huge, winged dragon perched there. Its massive tail slid sideways across the flagstone floor and recoiled lazily, recreating the shuffling noise the painter had heard earlier.

The dragon's eyes glowed dirty orange like embers. Sparks rose erratically from its mouth and nostrils, betraying the fire raging within its gullet. When the creature hissed, steamy dark slime dripped from its flared gills.

The painter fled panicked from the room and woke the castle with his warning cries. Knights rushed to their stations as the dragon, now in flight, circled the courtyard once and then disappeared into the night. When they examined the balcony with torchlight, they found black slime drying into tar-like clumps.

The next morning the painter set out with his canvas carefully wrapped for several days' journey. Since it was the dragon's work that had destroyed his painting, surely the Great King would know some remedy. He hastened to the encampment where the Great King was traveling with his armies. When he arrived, he wandered through the camp until he found the King leaning over maps with his captains, planning their battle strategies.

The painter suddenly felt foolish. Who was he to demand the Great King's time? He hung back at the edge of the field court and chastised himself. But then, he heard someone call his name.

Looking up, he saw that the King had left the group of captains and was coming toward him.

"What brings you here this long way?" asked the King with concern as he gripped the painter's shoulder in greeting.

"This." The painter fumbled to uncover his wretched canvas. He had once dreamed of unveiling the painting under very different circumstances.

The King eyed the canvas and heaved a deep sigh. "The dragon certainly left his sordid marks. But, who did this?" He pointed to the slashes made by the painter.

"I did, after I discovered the blotches . . ." the painter confessed with shame.

The King pursed his lips and nodded without condemnation. "No doubt, you have come here hoping I can tell you how to remove the dragon's marks. But, the remedy is far more powerful than that and will gaul the dragon to his very core."

"Tell me what this remedy is!" exclaimed the painter with relish.

"Come, let's walk," answered the King and they headed out of the encampment into a nearby meadow. "What do you see, my friend?"

"A grassy field. Hills and mountains in the distance," puzzled the painter.

Then the King drew him to stand beneath a strong oak tree at the field's edge. "Now what do you see?"

"The same as before, but through the low hanging boughs of this tree," answered the painter as leaves on the branches fluttered and danced before him in the breeze. When he grasped the King's vision for the marred canvas, the painter's face filled with excitement.

"It will take all of your artistic talent, and there will be times when you will feel like giving up before it is complete," warned the King compassionately. "But promise me, friend, that you will not slash the painting again yourself or abandon the project. If you give in to destruction, the dragon wins."

The painter agreed with renewed determination.

It was admired by all who saw it, a painting of exquisite depth and beauty. Those who looked on it felt as though they stood in the very place. The peaceful lake, graceful hills, and regal mountains were not viewed from some distant point. They were seen through swaying branches speckled with dark fluttering leaves.

When the dragon heard of it, he was incensed and still fumes over it to this day.

O   O   O

P e r s o n a l   R e f l e c t i o n

The Painting

✍ Parts of the parable that touched me are . . .

✍ When I read these parts I felt . . .

✍ Similar situations in my life are . . .

Your Life Is a Masterpiece: Using colored felt-tip pens or crayons, color the picture in which the blotches and slashes have become a meaningful part of the landscape. If this seems foolish, please do it to encourage the child within you. You might listen to some uplifting music as you color.

When have you felt the most hopeless about the circumstances in your life?

✍ _____

_____

Who or what has marred your painting?

✍ _____

_____

What has helped you cope with or transform the situation?

✍ _____

_____

Blotches: Being depressed does not mean we're crazy. Many of us feel depressed from time to time, particularly when we suffer some kind of emotional injury or loss. If you have thoughts of hurting or killing yourself, please call a local hotline to talk with someone who understands. The National Suicide Prevention Hotline at 1-800-333-4444 has counselors available twenty-four hours a day. Ask friends who have had counseling for the name of a good therapist. You might also consider having a physical examination, since some forms of depression have physical causes.

See Resources, page 181, for further help.

OGRE

o　　　o　　　o

"**A** rest would not be slovenly," said the old man, who leaned to a stop on his knotted cane. The woman beside him shifted the weight of the child sleeping in her arms and lowered herself onto a fallen log beside the forest path. It was an ideal height to sit on without having to bend the knees overmuch. Seats too low expended too much energy when the time to stand arrived. As the man sat also, the trunk sank slightly into the mossy ground.

"She is lovely," he said, looking at the child. Fast asleep with a peaceful pout on her lips, the child *was* beautiful. But it was a compliment the mother rarely heard because most people only noticed the little girl's twisted arms and legs.

"I wonder if the Great King will make her well instantly; or is it a thing that happens gradually just by living in his land?" The mother brushed one finger along her daughter's feathery brow.

"I've heard it told both ways, but more often gradual. Some say that once you're in his kingdom you forget about whatever brought you, and then one day realize you've become whole," said the old man in quiet awe.

"The reason for my sojourn is obvious, but why do you travel to the city of the Great King?" asked the woman.

Stroking his grayed beard as though it were a favorite cat, the aged man spoke with longing. "I remember how the sun once shone before the sorcerer's dark clouds covered everything with damp and drizzle. And I've heard there are no ogres in the Great King's land. One can live there in sunlight and without fear of beastly attack." He turned his head to search the tall ferns waving behind them and to reassure himself that only dark tree trunks stood there.

"People in my village laughed when I left. They think me a foolish widow because they don't believe the Great King exists. And there are times I doubt it myself," said the woman tiredly.

"It's not easy to seek what we've never seen," sighed the old man.

"I am glad we met on the road two days ago. Your company is a comfort on such a long journey."

"Aye. I only wish I were younger so I could defend us all from any evil we might meet. We'd best be on the way again." He rose from the log and glanced around uneasily once more.

They would need to find some rocks or an overhang before dusk to shelter them from the wet night air. Rocks to their back and a fire between them and the forest would also afford protection from anything hungry lurking in the dark. Nights were the hardest for the old man, for even after the ominous shadows in the woods faded into sleep, his dreams were invaded by loathsome ogres. They stood twice the size of men, with lanky arms hanging nearly to the ground, gaping mouths with spiked teeth, and mottled, hairless skin like slimy toads. He would run desperately from their long, clutching, fingers, waking with a choked scream just as he felt the clammy hands ensnare him. He was weary and tired from the life-long fear. The thought of nightfall approaching brought dread to his soul.

"Look, there ahead on the rise." The woman's excitement stirred the child in her arms. The path rose before them and divided, with one way winding to a wooded knoll. Glistening in the dim afternoon light was an ornate bronze gate of majestic height. Rushing toward it, their hearts were filled with joy. "Surely this is the entrance to the Great King's land!" exclaimed the woman, holding her wakened child on her hip.

"I thought we had much further to go," said the old man, glad to be at his journey's end. Inside the gateway, they found the wood thinned. Elegant ferns grew freely without brambles to quell them, and wild flowers of wonderful beauty blossomed all around. That night the old man slept peacefully without dream or terror.

After traveling in the new land nearly a week, they still had not come to any village or met any other traveler. Their food supplies grew scarce, and they took to eating wild berries growing in the woods. The berries were bitter but better than hunger. Then on the sixth day the path ended abruptly. It simply stopped in a thick wood.

"We've been cruelly tricked," said the woman.

"I fear you speak aright." The old man was heartsick. "We must return the way we came. The gate was, no doubt, a false one constructed by the sorcerer to lure travelers off the true path."

"But, how shall we know the real gate when we find it? The sorcerer may have more than one counterfeit."

"I wish I knew," confessed the old man.

The journey back seemed twice as long since they no longer traveled with hope. Once again on the original road, they came, after some time, to another offshoot and another gate, this one even more regal than the first.

Standing before it, they eyed the structure suspiciously.

"Has the same feel as the first one," said the woman.

"Aye," agreed the man, and so they bypassed it.

A few days later, the next gate was not of bronze, but an archway of vining flowers with royal banners flapping on posts at either side. However, their hopes were dashed once more when after a fortnight of journey the path fell off into a chasm. Sorely disheartened, they backtracked again.

"I cannot continue," cried the woman when they reached the main road. "Better my child live out her days at home, crippled, than die here for lack of nourishment. These berries give no sustenance. Look, your clothes hang on you loosely. We are wasting away."

"I beseech you, good woman, don't turn back yet. Come with me to whatever gate is next. If that be false, then I shall return with you and forget this quest." Seeing the fervor in his face, she reluctantly agreed.

After many days' travel the path eventually came to another gateway at dusk. This one was roughly hewn of wood, two posts and a crossbeam, that was all. The landscape looked no different on the other side from where they stood, but when they sampled the berries they found them sweet and so were heartened. Before evening fell they crossed a stream, chose a sheltered spot, and gathered wood for fire.

As was her custom, the mother sang as she rocked her child to sleep, but tonight the old man silenced her with an outstretched hand and apprehension on his face. They heard a rustling of leaves, but the wind seemed still. He saw the woman's face blanch as she clutched the child in terror. An ogre's bellow, like an enraged bull, shook the forest.

The old man's lungs felt like stones within his chest as he shouted, "Run for the stream we forded and go to the other side. Ogres abhor water and won't cross it. Go! Now!"

Grabbing a brand from the fire, he faced the darkness and saw a creature even more horrible than his nightmares. Its mouth, filled with jagged teeth, opened into a crooked leer. Drool hung like cobwebs from its chin. The ogre was as tall as the trees and broke lofty branches as it hunkered over to observe its prey. In his nightmares the old man had always run, but now in reality he stood his ground and raised the fiery brand above his head. It flew from his grasp with a bat from the ogre's massive hand and the old man was lifted into the air. Dangling him by one arm high above its head, the ogre bellowed again and then lowered him into its cavernous mouth.

The old man tumbled and slid in hideous slime, past the huge teeth and down a steep tunnel into the creature's rancid bowels. Enveloped in the humid darkness, he felt as though he would smother from the stench.

"Better to be torn limb from limb than to die slowly in this place!" he wailed and heard the ogre bellow all around him. The fleshy walls suddenly constricted and squeezed him tightly. He flailed in desperation and heard trees falling in the forest. The crushing pain intensified to an unbearable point and then suddenly ceased.

The old man opened his eyes to see the moonlit forest. He lay among the fallen trees, but the ogre was nowhere in sight. Standing shakily, he reached for the branch of a sapling to steady himself and stared at the hand that stretched out. It was young and strong and human. His chest was wide and muscular. He felt his face and found his beard still there, but looking down saw that it was no longer gray but brown.

Throwing his head back, he laughed uproariously and yelled aloud, "I thought he was squeezing the life out of me, but what I felt was his giant body conforming to my bones. I've taken his body and strength for my own!"

Picking up his knotted staff, he went to find the woman and child and came upon them at the stream. They sat on the other bank, weeping.

"Good woman, do not mourn. This is indeed the land of the Great King!" he called out.

The woman paused, staring at him with angry distrust. "You are either mistaken or a liar, tall stranger."

"Look at the moonlight! When have you ever seen it so bright? There are no clouds obscuring it! And look at me. I am your traveling companion, victorious over the ogre!" he pronounced exuberantly and thrust his gnarled cane into the air like a battle sword.

"How can this be?" she asked warily, not at all convinced.

"The ogre overpowered my frail body, but once inside him I overpowered his mindless soul!" He splashed in the water in jubilant celebration, climbing onto her side of the embankment. Water ran in streams from the bottom tip of his dark beard. Then he shook his head like a dog to dry himself and grinned from ear to ear. "Is it not wondrous?"

"Wondrous indeed!" Recognizing her friend's voice and seeing his eyes in the face, she embraced him gladly.

o   o   o

P e r s o n a l   R e f l e c t i o n

Ogre

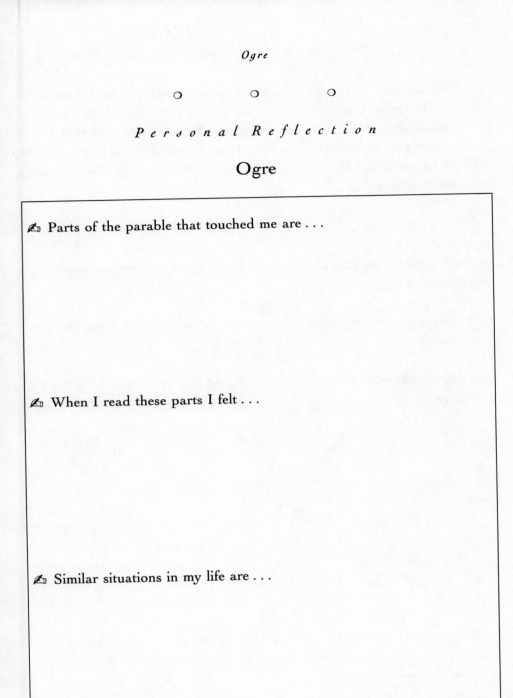

✍ Parts of the parable that touched me are . . .

✍ When I read these parts I felt . . .

✍ Similar situations in my life are . . .

Although at times we feel swallowed up by our ogres, they will not annihilate us. In the end, we find that we are more powerful than the ogres.

Below, list some of the ogres in your life. These could be traumatic events from your past or fears you have in the present or behavior that stops you from living a balanced life. Next to each ogre, list how you would like to emerge stronger from facing it.

Ogres in My Life	*How I Would Like to Emerge Stronger from Facing My Ogre*
✍ Overcontrolling because I fear powerlessness	✍ Being an effective manager
Excessive caretaking for fear of being selfish	Having sensitivity for others *and* for myself
Repressing childhood abuse memories	Facing what happened and grieving over it so I don't allow continued abuse
✍	✍

Naming our ogres is a lot like doing a fourth step in a Twelve-Step recovery program, in which we make a moral inventory of ourselves, including both our good and our bad points. See Appendix 2, page 175, for more information on the Twelve Steps.

*H*is sisters and younger brother sat silently at the wooden table as the boy and his father, smudged with soot and sweat, tramped into the cottage. The father, renowned for his feats of strength, was a big man with wide shoulders and massive arms well suited to his trade as blacksmith. It was sometimes rumored in the village that this man was half troll. But no one ever voiced such an accusation within his hearing. The lad took his seat without a word and watched his mother carefully fill their bowls, starting with the head of the household.

"None for him," growled the father when the mother reached for the boy's dish. "He was good for nothing today. Spooked the horse I was shoeing so the beast nearly kicked my head in."

Face reddening, the son opened his mouth to protest. Before any words had a chance to emerge he felt the urgent nudging of his older sister's foot. Her eyes pleading for silence, she secretly drew a bread roll from her pocket and placed it in his lap under the table. He quickly hid it in the folds of his shirt, thankful that he would not go to bed hungry tonight. But, for now, his stomach gnawed as he smelled the stew's meaty aroma and watched the others eat.

His mother poured drink for each one. Then, wiping her hands nervously on her apron, she sat down with the family. The father was in one of those moods tonight. Hunkered over his food like a bear, he chewed slowly, and his eyes watched every move at the table. The children ate carefully, knowing that even the smallest of indiscretions might unleash his day's pent-up anger.

The youngest child broke the uneasy tension. "Father, did you shoe the Great King's war horse today? Did you see the Great King?" Her cheerful chatter sometimes disarmed the father's brewing temper.

"Was a hasty messenger for the King whose horse threw a shoe. Don't care to see the Great King himself, for we were better off before he came. Forging swords for the sorcerer brought more food to this table than shaping horseshoes and plowshares. Talk of the land is how the Great King's routed the sorcerer, backed him to the sea and freed us. But, I hear the magician has called on help from his lord, the dragon. So, the final battle is yet to be fought."

"But, isn't the Great King more powerful than the dragon and sorcerer together?" asked the youngest child.

"If the Great King has the power and might, why hasn't he slain the dragon before now, eh? Sorcerers, they come and go, but not the dragon. We'll be worse off with him about, you can be sure of that."

"How will it be worse?" The little girl gave her full attention to her father while the family exchanged furtive glances, hoping this discourse would last through supper until they could each escape to chores and bed.

"You think a cloudy sky and trolls bandying about collecting the sorcerer's taxes was bad? Well, the dragon don't want no coins. He craves human flesh. He'll torch this thatched roof some night and carry off the worthless lot of you for a feast. Worthless lot of you." He sank into sullen silence once more and drank his cup dry.

"Bring me more," he demanded, eyeing his youngest son. The little boy dutifully fetched the pitcher and refilled his father's cup. "Can you speak yet without halting?"

Not meeting his father's eyes, the little boy shook his head.

"Answer me with a word!"

"N-n-no, sire," stuttered the child.

"Dung for brains," said the father with disgust, and he cuffed the side of the boy's head so violently that the child fell against the wall. Apparently, the night's victim had been chosen.

"At least he's got brains," murmured the older son, hoping to bait his father away from beating the little brother.

"Say what?" the father asked evenly without raising his voice. But his eyes were like steel. No one in the room breathed for a moment. Rising to his feet, the smithy swung a huge arm across the length of the table and slapped his oldest son. The blow knocked the youth from his seat onto the flagstone floor.

At least the waiting is over, the boy thought to himself as his father strode to stand over him and land a series of painful kicks. He was strangely aware of the faces of his family during the beatings. His mother always stood alone, biting her lower lip. The older sister comforted the crying little sister. And the younger brother stared vacantly as if he neither saw nor heard at all.

As for himself, he somehow blocked out the impact of the blows. His body never hurt until later, after his father stopped and went to his bedroom bellowing, "Woman, come to bed and leave the children to clean up the meal."

Then, when the boy picked himself up off the floor, he felt the pain. His older sister pressed a wet cloth against his face to stop the bleeding, but he pulled away angrily.

"Don't coddle me. I'm not a baby!" He gingerly fingered his mouth and was relieved to find his teeth in place. The older sister had not been so fortunate the last time she was beaten. Whenever she smiled now, she self-consciously put a hand to her mouth to cover the gap on one side in her upper row of teeth.

"Did you spook the horse on purpose so it would kick Father?" asked the youngest child incredulously.

"No, dullard. The horse reared when I sneezed. But, some day I will kill him. I will," the boy vowed with conviction.

"You mustn't say that," scolded his older sister. "He is our father. If we all tried harder to do well he wouldn't be so cross. We must all try harder."

"Try harder? What tripe you speak! I'll try harder to hasten his death, that's all."

"Please don't kill Father, for then we shall all be orphans and die of starvation in the street," wailed the youngest child.

"Now look what you've done. You've brought her to tears." The older sister turned to lift the little girl into her arms. "There, there. Hush now. Let me see your pretty smile and cheer us with a happy laugh. Yes, that's what I like to see."

"You want him dead, don't you?" He slapped the back of his hand against his younger brother's shoulder. The little boy said nothing, but shrugged apathetically.

"Why do I waste my time with you all? You act as if I am the villain, not he!" the older brother accused them.

"You do stir him up. If I hadn't quieted you at the table tonight you would have argued over the stew. We try to keep you from the beatings, but you won't heed us."

"I see." The boy glared at his sister.

"Look at me. Look at me!" interrupted the youngest child walking between them with a bowl gaily balanced on her head. The boy angrily batted the dish off. The older sister barely caught the bowl in time to save it from smashing on the hearth.

"Stop your meanness!" the older sister complained to her brother. "We would all get a beating if he found a bowl broken. You make it harder for us all!"

"No longer. Fare for yourselves. Find out, dear sister, if trying harder improves his countenance. Smile and laugh, little sister, perhaps you can waylay his temper. Brother, draw no attention to yourself by word or action and, perhaps, he will forget you are even here. I leave you to your own devices. As for me, I shall find the Great King's army and join its ranks as a page. Then, when I am old enough to be a warrior I shall kill ten thousand trolls in battle before returning here to lop off Father's head. When next he sees me, it shall be his death!"

Filtered through purple silk overhead, the light in the Great King's field tent had an early morning cast, even though the midday sun shone bright outside. A hand to his chin and one finger against his lips, the Great King reclined between the arms of a carved, high-backed chair. "You requested this private audience to defend your name. I am told that for the fourth time this month you have quarreled with other pages and come to blows. What have you to say for yourself?"

"I'm tall enough to be a warrior now. They're jealous that I shall be over them soon," the smithy's son explained confidently. "The captain of the guard sides with them, but I knew I would receive a fair hearing from you."

"Readiness to be a warrior requires more than stature," said the King.

"I am strong. No one prevails against me. Already I can stay the knights in sword practice. Why am I not advanced from serving as a page?"

"I know your skill full well. In the year you have been with us, you have grown in every way except that which is most needed," the King said with sadness. "And, in this, you have resisted instruction."

The young man held his tongue while anger surged black within him.

"You have the temper of a child," continued the King. As he spoke he rose from his chair. "You stir up strife wherever you go."

"My Lord, it's true the fire within me burns hotter than for most. But, let me pour the searing coals I carry upon the heads of the King's enemies in battle. Then I shall not be continually consumed."

"I wish it could be so, my son. But, that is not the nature of fire. Once fanned in battle, your temper would afterward be more inflamed than ever." The King grasped the smithy's son by one shoulder and looked long into his eyes. "Do you desire to serve me?" the King asked gently.

"Yes, Sire. You know I do," the youth pledged fervently.

"Then you must be willing to overcome this defect of character. You must tame the troll blood in your veins."

All his life he had bludgeoned anyone who dared to make such an accusation of heritage. He had always guessed it was true, but still the King's words galled him. "Am I supposed never to feel angry?" His voice quavered with emotion, and he fought to force it back under his control.

"There is nothing wrong with anger. Men choose what they shall do with it. They choose whether to use their indignation for right or wrong. A troll, however, flares up into anger at any excuse. With no thought for his course of action, he lashes out. To tame this, you must go on a journey you will not want to take: You must go home."

"Home?" he exclaimed, at first dismayed, but then heartened by a new thought. "Am I to kill my father?"

"You will know what to do when the time comes." Opening a small wooden chest, the King removed a pendant of rare worth and value. The amethyst gemstone, surrounded by an oval of finely crafted silver, hung on a sturdy chain. Slipping it over the young man's head, the King pronounced, "You will need this for your journey."

As he crested the hill of the road leaving the King's encampment, the young man turned to look back at the vast array of tents. Further in the distance, dismal clouds overhung the sorcerer's fortress on the sea cliffs. He hoped the long siege would continue until his return so that he could be among the warriors who overtook the stronghold. Turning back to the road, the youth fingered the gem as he walked and marveled that the King would bestow such a treasure on him.

Not long into the journey, an old man passed going the opposite direction with a herd of unruly sheep. Try as he might to avoid the animals, the smithy's son was bumped and nudged and nearly knocked over. As if this was not irritation enough, he then caught a glimpse of the old shepherd chuckling at his predicament. Enraged, the youth pushed through the bleating animals, intending to throttle the herdsman. His chest became hot, he thought from the exertion. But then just as his hands encircled the elderly shepherd's throat, he realized that the heat was searing in one spot on his skin. Looking down, he saw the pendant glowing like a red-hot coal. Releasing the bug-eyed man, the youth grabbed at the chain to pull the burning gem away from his skin. The shaken herdsman hurried on to catch up with his animals, leaving the young man to watch the gem quickly return to its normal state. When he thought of going after the mocker, the pendant grew hot again.

One cold night he stopped to eat and warm himself at a crowded and noisy inn. As he lifted a spoonful of soup to his lips, someone jostled him from behind and the liquid splattered. The young man stood angrily and focused steely eyes on the bumbler. Once more the pendant burned unbearably upon his chest, and reflexively, he bent forward so it would hang away from his skin. This brought him eye to eye with the short farmer who had stumbled against him. "Watch where you're going next time," growled the young man, deciding not to pummel the offender's face. Instantly, he felt the gem cool.

Some days later the road passed through an orchard filled with busy harvesters. As the young man walked by, an apple careened through the air and hit him on the shoulder. Furious, he drew his sword to face the attacker and saw a youth not much younger than himself perched wide-eyed in a nearby tree.

"Beg your pardon. I didn't see you, I swear. It was meant for him." He pointed to a giggling cohort across the road. The pendant heated from his anger as the smithy's son stooped and picked up the apple. Then, smiling he brushed the apple on his shirt and broke into laughter, realizing the ridiculousness of his original intention to lop off someone's head.

Suddenly, his jacket began to feel heavy. To his amazement, small gemstones poured forth from the pockets like beans from an open sack. The harvesters gawked as he dropped the apple and gathered the spilled treasure in his hands. With bulging pockets he proceeded on in wonderment.

In the next village, the smithy's son sought out the miller to buy a sack. It seemed a wiser way to carry the precious stones, rather than let the bulge in his pockets call attention to his new wealth. But word of the gemstones traveled. The next day he was accosted by thieves on the road. Throwing off one who had jumped him from the bushes, he drew his sword and ran through the one coming at him with a club. Fury surged in his veins. Even as the sword sank into its target, the smithy's son felt a tug behind him and saw the first assailant running off with the sack. Outraged, he pursued the thief and managed to throw him to the ground.

"You shall die like your friend," he snarled to the man who struggled under his hold. Suddenly, the pendant heated to burning. The young man pulled the blade away from the thief's throat to consider the matter. The pendant had made no protest during the fray when he fought to defend himself. But now, the remaining attacker was subdued. Nonetheless, the man deserved death. He moved his blade against the neck once more and felt the pendant sear. Although it vexed him greatly, he knew what was called for. So he tied the thief to a tree and alerted the next village as to where the criminal could be found.

In that town he bought some fine clothes to replace those torn in the melee. He purchased also a good horse to carry him more quickly on his way. In a short time, he would reach his father's village.

○   ○   ○

Personal Reflection

Troll House I

🖎 Parts of the parable that touched me are . . .

🖎 When I read these parts I felt . . .

🖎 Similar situations in my life are . . .

The Pendant in My Life: The pendant represents self-awareness about our emotions and behavior. Self-awareness allows us to make choices rather than blindly react. Relating to ourselves and others in a healthier way enriches us like gemstones pouring out of our pockets.

If I had a magic pendant, it would help me be aware of my behavior regarding . . .

I can make choices about my behavior by . . .

You may have recognized the dysfunctional family roles of the smithy's children; the over-responsible family hero (oldest daughter); the angry, trouble-making scapegoat (oldest son); the quiet, lost child (younger son); and the tension-relieving placater (younger daughter). What kind of role or combination of roles did you and your siblings have in your family?

✍

_____

_____

_____

_____

_____

_____

_____

_____

_____

_____

_____

_____

As we grow in recovery, we are sent on a journey we might not want to take, a journey home in the sense of examining what happened in our families so that we can get beyond it. See Resources, page 177, for helpful books about exploring dysfunctional families.

TROLL HOUSE II

○   ○   ○

*A*s the young man approached the cottage behind the blacksmith shop, he heard the clanging of his father's hammer pounding out hot metal on the anvil. The pendant heated inconveniently as he pictured caving in his father's head with the same hammer. But before going to the shop, he would visit his family.

When he opened the door, his mother and sisters stood apprehensively. Some of the string beans they had been snapping fell from their laps.

"What business have you here, sir?" challenged his older sister, for they did not recognize him.

"I have business to see my mother and sisters," the smithy's son replied.

The youngest sister burst into a smile and ran to embrace him. She was grown far more than he expected, but he still easily whisked her into the air in greeting.

"Where is my brother?" he asked, setting her down.

Her smile faded. "He left some months ago after Father found the old skins he'd been hiding and using for parchment. He liked to write lots of words. Father beat him when he found the parchments and threw them all in the fire to break him of such foolishness. We've heard nothing from him since he left. He didn't even say good-bye."

The heat of the pendant flared on his chest with newly fanned murderous thoughts toward his father.

"You musn't let Father know you're here," pleaded the older sister. "He blames all his ills on you, even more so since you left, for he is overworked without your help. Please leave. He will be furious if he sees you."

"You needn't fear his temper any longer," said the brother, pouring a sack of glistening jewels onto the coarse wooden table. He had laughed at his own brashness several times on the trip and so the treasure had multiplied. "I will take care of you all now. Come away with me." He gently embraced his trembling mother. "There is no need to live any longer in fear. Pack what you want, all of you, and let us be gone."

His mother backed away from him slowly, her eyes averted, and shook her head. "I cannot leave your father. It would not be right. He is a good man who works hard to provide for us."

"A good man? Only in comparison to your own father who drank too much ale to work. You deserve far better than either of them, Mother." He reached out a hand to her. "Come away with me."

"No, I cannot leave your father," she whispered. Wringing her hands, she fled the room.

"I will not leave Mother. She is too frail to run the household by herself," asserted the older sister. "Now, please. go before he finds you here."

"I'm not going anywhere until you speak with her and convince her to come. She always listens to you."

"No, I won't badger her. Look at what you're doing. Just as before, you're always upsetting everyone!" The sister's face turned red with emotion.

"Let's play hide and seek like we used to!" exclaimed the little sister, pushing between her two angry siblings. "Wouldn't that be great fun?"

"Shut up!" snarled the brother.

"I'll play hide and seek with you, dearest," said the older sister, gathering the child into her arms and glaring furiously at the brother.

"Will you stay or go?" he huffed at the little girl.

"You're always so cross with me. I don't want to go with you," she said with her lower lip protruding.

He pushed a hand to his forehead in exasperation. "Very well. I won't press either of you to come. But I will leave these jewels so your life will be easier."

"No, Brother. Take them with you or Father will want to know where they came from. He would throw the pouch in the river rather than take charity from you." The older sister busily scooped the gems into the pouch and pushed it toward him.

He felt like telling them they were fools, but instead he said, "I will bury these in the ground on the north side of the gnarled tree." It was a tree they had often climbed, behind the cottage. "Some day, when you need the jewels they will be waiting for you."

"Do whatever you wish with them. But leave now before Father spies your horse and comes to see who is here."

Taking leave with angry disappointment, the smithy's son buried the jewels as he had promised. Then he went to his horse and pried off one of its shoes.

The pendant under his shirt grew hot as he led the animal to the front of the smithy's shop. Only a few people passed him, for the shop and cottage were the last buildings at the end of the village road. The large double doors stood open and the smells of his childhood rushed out. He could see his father at the back pouring melted alloys into molds and the pendant on his chest felt as hot.

"Morning, sir," his father greeted him somberly, without smiling. "What have you need of?" Like the others, he did not recognize the traveler.

For a moment, looking into the hated face, the son had no words. "Horse lost a shoe," he finally said.

"Let's have a look," said the smithy, lifting the horse's hoof. As the father bent over, the son thought how easily he could draw his sword and sever the man's arrogant head from his body. He gasped with the sudden intense pain from the pendant and leaned forward to move it away from his skin. "You ailing?" inquired the smithy.

"Old wounds," said the son.

The smithy guffawed as he worked on the shoe. "Surely you're too young to have battle wounds."

"I was attacked by a troll in my youth," the son spoke through clenched teeth, his eyes riveted on the smithy.

"Not many live to tell of such."

"I was fortunate to survive," asserted the son. "And fortunate to come into great wealth. I have need of a strong man such as yourself. The place of work is far from here. You cannot take your family, but you shall be richer than you ever dreamed." He poured gems from another pouch into his hand and held it out to the smithy. The man's bushy eyebrows pulled together, and he searched the traveler's face suspiciously.

"For a goose chase, why should I abandon them who depends on me?"

"I will give you the bag of jewels now, only you must agree to live out your life where I send you. Before you leave, I will give your family an equal amount. They shall never want for anything," the son countered.

"What trickery you devise I do not know. But, I will tell you this. Only a cur would leave his family, jewels or no jewels. You best take your offer elsewhere."

The shoeing was finished. The son, determined to rid his family of their tormentor, agonized over what he was about to do.

"Let me pay for your work with this pendant." He pulled the chain over his head and placed it around his father's neck. Raising his eyebrows, the smithy examined it with interest.

"Wear it always and you shall find your troll nature quelled. I know, because it helped me, Father."

"Father?" spit the smithy as he realized who the traveler was and became livid. Without warning he lunged for a choke hold on the son's throat. The searing of the pendant enraged him further and interrupted his attack. Wrenching it from his neck, he flung it into the straw on the floor. The two men circled each other, crouching with arms ready for violence. The son retrieved the pendent at his feet without taking his eyes off the father and slipped it once more over his own neck.

"Did you think to murder me so easily with that accursed pendant? You shall be the one to die! From your birth, you have been ungrateful. I rue the day I spawned you. You are a constant nettle in my flesh! I would have drowned you when I first laid eyes on you but for your mother's pleading. My mercy only brought suffering for her all these years. You have been the bane of our existence!"

"Was I everything troll you loathed in yourself? Look closely at your memories, Father. Was I not just like you?"

The smithy's lips curled in disdain, and he swung to hit his son in the jaw. But the young man dodged the fist and was surprised to find himself laughing.

"You have no power over me anymore! No power to beat me. No power to make me hate you. You may have the physical strength of ten men, but inside you are a weak and pitiful man! I am freed of you!" His pockets bulged to overflowing and such an array of jewels poured forth that the two men stood ankle deep in gems.

"What sorcery is this?" The father backed angrily out of the jewels, for they cut him like shards of glass. "Come against me fairly and we shall see who stands in the end. Let us fight to the death and end this enmity once and for all!"

"It is already ended," said the son. And knowing what to do, he mounted his horse and rode away.

○   ○   ○

P e r s o n a l   R e f l e c t i o n

Troll House II

✎ Parts of the parable that touched me are . . .

✎ When I read these parts I felt . . .

✎ Similar situations in my life are . . .

When we experience growth and change we want to share some of this new treasure with family members. It is not uncommon for our families to cling to their old dysfunctional patterns. The best way to share our newfound treasure is simply to be healthy despite family pressures. We are responsible only for our own recovery.

How I Used To Act with Family Members	*How I Can Be Different from My Old Role*
✍ I listen as Mom complains about Dad and never talk about my own life.	✍ Say, "I'm sorry you're upset with Dad, but let's talk about other things in our lives."
When I'm with my family at holidays, they drink beer and watch television. I just sit there bored.	I bring a favorite board game and invite those who would like to play. The others can watch television.
✍	✍

When we grow up in dysfunctional families, we must eventually deal with our anger and other strong feelings. Using a separate sheet of paper, write a letter to a parent, which you may or may not send. In this letter simply tell your parent how you have experienced your life, what you appreciated from them as well as what hurt you.

WISE ONES

o   o   o

*T*he quiet, youngest son of the blacksmith grew to manhood as he wandered through many lands searching for truth. All that he discovered and thought about he carried in his heart only, for scrolls and parchments do not travel well. Few were the people he met who pondered questions about life as he did. But he continued undaunted.

Sometimes at night when he slept, a dream came to him of a castle on the shore of a mountain lake bordered by magnificent peaks. It faded in and out of thick morning fog as he sailed toward it with deep longing in a roughly hewn boat. He always awakened from the dream with sadness and a renewed fervor in his quest.

He visited many places, but never stayed anywhere long until one day he came upon a small town different from the rest. He felt it when he met the first villager who was happily sweeping the cobbled square. One after another the people warmly greeted him as they contentedly carried out their tasks. Preparations were underway for a feast in the square.

"Will you stay and banquet with us, traveler?" asked one friendly man.

"Gladly," answered the blacksmith's son. "But, tell me, sir, who is this feast in honor of?"

"The Great King, of course," smiled the robust man.

"The Great King will be here?" inquired the blacksmith's son with interest, for many were the stories he had heard about this king.

"We are the people of the Great King, and we build the castle where he will reign." The man raised one arm grandly toward a knoll in the center of the village where the newly constructed foundation of a castle was visible.

"Teacher," a young woman addressed the man respectfully, "the meal is ready to be served." Then she smiled shyly at the smithy's son.

"Come, let us eat!" announced the man in a booming voice and then motioned the smithy's son to sit beside him. Young and old gathered at the many tables heaped with food in the square. "May you find sustenance here for both your body and your soul," said the friendly man as he passed a plate of steaming chicken to the traveler.

"I came here as you some months ago and have had no desire to leave," explained a young man sitting nearby. "The wise ones here know the answers to life and happiness. The greatest teacher among them has invited you to this meal. Truly, you are privileged today."

"But, where is the Great King?" asked the smithy's son curiously.

"He will dwell among us when his castle is finished," answered the teacher. "If you would like to meet him, you are welcome to stay and build with us."

"I fear I know nothing about stonework or carpentry."

"No knowledge is needed. Only a willing heart."

So the smithy's son stayed after the meal to help in the work on the castle. As the people labored, the wise ones took turns teaching lessons from various places in the castle. They spoke about life and relationships and inner peace. Their words were full of depth, and the smithy's son had much to ponder.

Each day after the evening meal, he sought out one of the wise ones to question him further.

"A mind searching for truth, this is a precious thirst you have," the teacher commended him. "Few are those who wrestle with the deeper things."

"But what did you mean when you said we must leave behind all we learned before coming here? Is truth too weak to exist elsewhere?"

"No," answered the wise one patiently. "Truth is powerful, but those without opened eyes cannot see. You are still blinded by your past, traveler, by the darkened household you grew up in." They sat with a handful of others around a hearth in one of the cottages.

"I notice a slight hesitation, a pause sometimes between your words," said the young man who had come to the village shortly before the smithy's son. "I wonder, did you stammer as a child?"

The smithy's son reddened. It was a handicap he had struggled long to overcome. He did not like to hear that it was still apparent.

"Do not be embarrassed," smiled the wise one. "We have all come here with frailties. This brother does not point this out to demean you, but to free you. He has already learned much in his time with us."

The brother beamed at the compliment and then continued his inquiry. "Who is the listener from your past who makes you choose your words so carefully?"

"My father," answered the smithy's son uneasily. He had the feeling this brother was more interested in looking wise than in caring for the souls of others.

"It is difficult for you to trust, even now," said the wise one, taking over. "We are not like your father. You may stutter here, and no one will think the less of you. Do you see, now, how you must forget what you have learned before coming to us? Cast aside the old. Think new thoughts. Be who you are without fear."

The others around the hearth nodded in agreement, each taking the teaching for themselves.

The castle walls rose slowly. The days were long, but the tedium of the labor was eased by the wise ones and their lectures. And by the shy, young woman the smithy's son had met at the feast that first day.

He helped her clean the food kettles after the evening meals, and then she helped him boil reeds for pulp to make into parchment. As he recorded the words of the wise ones, he taught her to read and write, for her mind was sharp and clear. He loved her and was sure the same ardor glowed in her eyes for him.

"I have never felt like I belonged anywhere until now," the smithy's son mused one evening as he walked her to the cottage she shared with other maidens. "In my own family, it was as if I were born into the wrong household full of people I had nothing in common with. But here, almost so slowly as to go unnoticed, I have come to feel a sense of kinship with all of you."

She squeezed his hand happily. "I thought I was content here before you came. But now I am truly satisfied."

He loved the way little wisps of hair always loosened themselves from her braids and hung lightly about her face.

The smithy's son took her other hand and pulled her to face him, "Be my wife."

She blushed, smiling. "We shall have to ask the wise ones."

"Why?"

"Because that is the way it is done here," she laughed embracing him.

"It is not the right time," answered the greatest of the wise ones. "You have not been one of us long enough yet, traveler."

Sorely disheartened, the smithy's son searched the wise one's face. "How many more months do you require for me to prove my steadfastness?" He imagined his love's disappointment when he would take her this news.

"It is not a matter of months. It is a matter of your heart. You still question us on what we teach just as you did at the beginning."

"And that displeases you?" asked the smithy's son, surprised.

"At some point you must stop wrestling with the truth and embrace it." The wise one looked piercingly into his eyes.

"But that is who I am. I think and question and ponder. It is my nature."

"No, it is your distrust that does these things. When you truly believe, you will rest in the truth," reassured the wise one.

From then on the smithy's son worked diligently at holding his tongue. The questions still arose in his mind, but he inwardly chastised himself for such faithless thinking and refused to give them voice. Strangely, the hesitancy and pause in his speech became more bothersome as he sought to purge his soul of its disloyalty. He stammered often and saw on the faces of his friends the slight winces and pity for his obvious discomfort. So he kept silent rather than expose his impairment.

Even with his love, he was often silent.

"What is wrong?" she asked with concern one evening.

"I fear I am a m-m-most unworthy subject of the Great King," he confessed to her. "And m-m-most unworthy to be your husband."

"Why do you have such thoughts? The wise ones are pleased with you and have given us permission now to marry in the fall. You should be happy, not sorrowful," she said gently.

The smithy's son looked into her eyes and wondered whether he dared to tell her the truth about his thoughts. He decided against it, for he knew what her response would be. She would insist he seek help from one of the wise ones. Yet, if they knew his real thoughts, they would not allow him to marry.

He was forced to live a lie if he wanted to be happy. Yet how could he be happy in such dishonesty, even if he were married to his love? Anguished of soul, he bid her goodnight and walked by himself. For some reason, thoughts of the mountain castle came to mind and he wondered why the dream had not come to him for a long while now. Outside the village he eyed the moonlit castle rising regally above the thatched roof cottages. The fortress did not sit on the edge of a lake. No peaks rose loftily behind it. Tomorrow the celebration for its completion would be held. But there was no rejoicing in the traveler's heart.

The people sang songs to the Great King as the wise ones took their seats on the thrones in the castle. The largest and most ornate chair in the center was occupied by the great teacher. He smiled benevolently as the villagers thronged in the huge room. When he stood to address them, an expectant hush fell over the adoring crowd.

"Truly, the enlightenment of the Great King is here with us today," announced the wisest of the wise ones. "And so shall he reign through us."

"When I first came here, you said the Great King himself would come to reign," said the smithy's son clearly, without a stammer.

Gasps of amazement and indignation filled the room. The future bride of the smithy's son looked at him aghast. Though her horror cut him to the quick, he strode up the steps of the dais and faced the villagers.

"Have you forgotten what the wise ones taught us when we started building the castle? They said it was for the Great King and that he would come here to reign. We all looked forward to meeting the Great King! But as the castle neared completion, the wise ones began teaching about the ideals of the Great King that would reign here through them. Do any of you secretly question this as I have over the past months? Do any of you yearn to meet the Great King as I do? He is not here. Only the wise ones sit on these thrones. Anyone who seeks the Great King must leave this place to find him."

Enraged, the crowd rushed on the smithy's son and beat him. He struggled to breathe through his mouth, for blood rushed from his nose down his throat.

"Stop!" commanded the greatest of the wise ones above the din of the mob. "My people, don't you see what he is doing? He has incited you to be abusive for that is what he knows. He turns you into his half-troll father!"

With the crowd temporarily restrained, the wise one descended from his throne to put a comforting arm around the tearful woman who loved the smithy's son.

"Let us love you," said the wise one to the traveler. "Put your past behind you."

"Don't push us away. Let the wise ones help you," pleaded the woman, reaching out to her beloved.

The smithy's son resolutely and slowly shook his head. Then pushing through the crowd, he left the castle, wiping the back of his sleeve across his bloodied face.

On the road outside the village, he headed toward the Northlands to search for the highest mountains.

○　　　○　　　○

Personal Reflection

Wise Ones

✍ Parts of the parable that touched me are . . .

✍ When I read these parts I felt . . .

✍ Similar situations in my life are . . .

Unhealthy groups have costly rules for membership: Don't talk or question. Don't trust yourself or anyone not in the group. Don't feel anything except what the group says you should be feeling.

What false Higher Power have you put your trust in? (This might be an unhealthy spiritual group, a psychotherapy cult, a bottle, a marriage.)

✍ _____

_____

_____

How did you come to realize that the power you found in your abusive or addictive system or substance was not real power?

✍ _____

_____

_____

How did this victimization affect your relationship with your Higher Power?

✍ _____

_____

_____

The traveler continued searching for truth after leaving the village. He did not give up his quest to find the Great King. How are you continuing your quest for personal growth?

✍ _____

_____

_____

See Resources, page 177, for a list of organizations to help in recovering from unhealthy groups.

Dance in the Dark

○　　○　　○

*T*he little princess fought back tears as she ran from the cousins and brothers chasing her. Ahead in the courtyard she saw her father and uncle evaluating the leg of an injured war horse. Seeking refuge between the two men, the princess pointed in terror to the approaching boys. "They have a snake!"

"Here now, you'll get trampled." Her father gruffly pulled her away from the startled horse.

"You boys," her uncle called out as he lifted the princess protectively into his arms. "Leave off!" One brother dangled the garden snake toward the princess for the thrill of a last screech from her, then the harassers ran away giggling.

"Why do they hate me so?" sobbed the princess.

"No, they *like* you. You're the prettiest princess in the castle. That's why they enjoy teasing you." Her uncle smiled.

"Then I'd rather be ugly so they'd leave me alone."

"You won't think so when you're older," assured her uncle.

"Cut his throat," the king somberly instructed the waiting groomsman, and the uncle's attention turned once more to the ailing horse.

"It's a shame he's not healing," commiserated the uncle.

"He was a fine charger, but no more," muttered the king brusquely as he walked away.

The princess sadly watched the great roan horse as it was led off and thought her father a very cruel man. "Why doesn't father have the grooms- man take the roan to the Great King? My nursemaid says that the Great King loves all creatures and cares for them."

"Does she now? Well, the Great King's land is a far way off. Too far to go. If the lame roan were mine, I'd probably keep him for a stud and let him sire fine colts for you to ride upon." Her uncle tickled her arm, and the laugh- ter almost made her forget about the poor horse's fate.

While the princess's father was weighted down and irritable with many things, her uncle always had time for her. He took her riding, carried her around the castle on his shoulders, sang her songs, and told her stories. No one except her nursemaid pampered the princess more than her uncle. She thought him the most wonderful person alive, for everything was always fun when her uncle joined in.

He was her mother's youngest brother and could have his pick of any of the ladies of the land to marry, but he had not chosen yet. "There are too many beautiful flowers," she once overheard him say. "Why should I choose only one when I enjoy them all?"

Sometimes late at night when everyone in the castle slept, her uncle would come to her chambers and rouse her to play hide and seek in the moon- lit rooms. It was great fun to creep about, stifling giggles so as not to waken the nursemaid snoring loudly in the adjoining room.

One night during their game the princess searched behind the large carved chest in the corner. She was startled when the heavy lid suddenly flew open, and her uncle emerged laughing.

"How did you get in there?" she whispered in amazement, for the chest had always been locked.

"There is nothing locked for me," grinned her uncle with raised eyebrows. "Look what treasures are here. Gold and silver and fine jewels given to you at your birth by well-wishers. Some day these will be part of your dowry. But this, this is the greatest treasure of all!" He pulled from a velvet sack a delicate gown that took the princess's breath away. It shimmered in the moonlight, and the princess gazed at it wide eyed. "Put it on," invited her uncle. "It is magic and was given to you by the fairies on the day of your birth."

"But, it is far too big to have fit me as a baby," puzzled the princess as the uncle put the dress over her head.

"It is the gown spun for your betrothal night," her uncle explained.

"Then I must not wear it now. Mother told me it is special for when I marry."

"My sister doesn't want you to wear it because she knows the power of its magic to make its wearer even more beautiful, and she is already jealous of you as it is."

"Mother is jealous of me?" asked the little girl as she pushed the too-long sleeves up her arms.

"Of course, my princess. She has long been the most beautiful woman in the land. Your older sisters, well, unfortunately, they favor your father's side. But, you, my princess, everyone can see that you will surpass your mother. Now come, let's dance!" He lifted her up on his hip as he whirled about the room, and the long gown flowed out in an ever changing glow of soft, magical colors.

As they danced he touched her in ways that only husbands should touch wives, but the little princess didn't know about such things. She found it hard to breath as he held her tighter and tighter in the wild whirling around the room. "Stop!" she whispered pushing her small arms against his chest. The uncle seemed not to hear. He continued his feverish dance until the princess was dizzy and called out as loudly as she dared for fear of waking the nursemaid.

Her uncle came to a sudden standstill as he caught his breath, "What magic you have in this gown, my princess! No man in the kingdom will be able to resist your charms! You shall have whatever you desire at the crook of your finger! But, no one must know that you have worn the dress, or they will be angry with you."

After that when her uncle came to her room at night he would not play hide and seek with her until she first put on the gown. Although the dancing made her dizzy and sick, she withstood it in order to get to her favorite game. It was much the same as her nursemaid who made her eat peas and lentils before she could have any sweetcake.

Even as she grew older and childhood games no longer held their sway, her uncle continued to creep to her chambers when everyone slept. Sometimes, in hopes that he would go away, she acted as though she slumbered too deeply to wake, but he would still wrap the gown around her and whisk her about the room. Other nights she tried to dissuade him saying, "Let's just play hide and seek like we used to. I don't want to dance tonight."

"Hide and seek is a child's game," winked her uncle. "You will soon be a beautiful woman and must know how to dance. Nothing brings me greater pleasure than these nights with you, for your magic pulls me here and is stronger than I can resist."

"I don't want to dance," the princess repeated adamantly, but the disappointment on her uncle's face was so great that she reluctantly gave in to his wishes. After each tryst the gown was crumpled into its velvet bag and hidden again in the darkness of the huge, carved chest.

In the great hall the dressmaker proudly shook out a bolt of material for display, "And this is the finest purple in the land!"

"Yes," agreed the queen appreciatively, and two of the older princesses eyed the material hungrily.

"Mother, this will look far better on me than her. See?" The dark-haired princess draped the material across her shoulders with regal aplomb.

"I think not!" protested the other sister, who snatched it away.

"No more of this!" pronounced the queen. "Is this the way princesses should behave? I am ashamed of you both. No, this purple shall be for your little sister's dress."

The youngest princess shook her head quickly as the two older sisters turned jealous eyes upon her. "Please, Mother, I prefer the gray brocade."

"I am tired of all the dull colors you wear, child. You are becoming a woman. It is time for color and gaiety."

"I don't want a purple dress," the princess protested. But her mother, already busy choosing material for her own new gown, ignored her.

"I won't wear it!" the young girl blurted with angry tears. She fled without waiting for her mother's reaction.

She ran to her rooms crying and found her nursemaid there cleaning.

"My Lady, what has so upset you?" asked the old woman as she put aside her dust cloth and took the princess in her arms.

"Mother is going to make me wear a purple dress," sobbed the child. The ample folds of the old woman's smock were filled with the smell of comfort and safety.

"Tell me why you don't like the purple. Perhaps I can intercede for you with the queen," said the nursemaid loudly, for in her old age she was losing her hearing.

"It's too bright. It's horrible. Men would all notice me and then wouldn't leave me alone," explained the princess.

"How would the men bother you?" asked the nursemaid with concern. Suddenly the princess feared she had revealed too much.

"You know how men are." The princess pulled away without looking into the nursemaid's eyes. "I must go now, but you will talk to my mother for me?" She glanced back at the nodding nursemaid before leaving.

"*Shall* we dance fast or slow?" asked her uncle that night. She hated that question. The faster pace was more sickening, but at least it was over quicker and not dragged out.

"Fast," she answered.

"That is my favorite also," smiled her uncle. "You and I are so much alike, my princess."

Suddenly, in the midst of their dance, torchlight filled the room, and the princess screamed as palace guards roughly seized her uncle.

"It's alright," cried the nursemaid clutching the princess to her chest. "If only I had realized earlier, my poor child. Everything will be alright now."

But the princess was terrified to see her uncle being taken away by the guards. She could see the panic he was thinly masking with his angry protests. He knew what would happen when her father found out.

"You're safe now," the nursemaid attempted to comfort her.

The princess struggled to be free of the nursemaid's embrace. "Let me go! I have to speak to my father before it's too late!"

By the time she reached her father's chambers, he had already been informed. She heard his enraged voice even before she entered the room where her mother pleaded with him.

"Please, do not do this thing! He is my only brother!" The queen attempted unsuccessfully to catch the king's arm as he angrily paced the length of the room.

"He will be beheaded in the courtyard at dawn's light!" the king repeated his decision.

"Father, it was my fault. If I hadn't put on the gown, he wouldn't have danced with me. Please don't hurt him. I'm to blame," the princess begged tearfully.

"There! Listen to your daughter if you will not listen to me," challenged the queen.

The king stopped his angry pacing to eye the two with disgust. "Very well then. He shall be banished. If ever he sets foot in this kingdom again his life shall be forfeited. Now leave me—both of you. And this shall never be spoken of again! Do you hear me?!"

They bowed obediently and backed out of the chamber.

"How could you let this happen?" The queen's eyes were like daggers piercing her daughter in the hallway. "Go to your room, and take that filthy thing off! Have you no decency?" she said before turning away and closing herself in her chambers. Alone in the torchlit hall, the princess looked down at the gown and gasped.

The delicate material was soiled and torn from the many nights of dancing. Its glow was now dingy and faint. The frayed hem of the gown, still too long for a young girl, dragged on the uneven edges of the stone floor as the princess returned, weeping, to her own rooms.

Her nursemaid was tearfully packing a patched sack there. "I have to go in the morning, my Lady." She hugged the princess tightly. "Your parents have dismissed me for letting such a thing happen while I slept. A nursemaid not so hard of hearing would have protected you far better. Besides, you are nearly the age now for attendants and don't need an old nursemaid any longer."

"Don't leave me," begged the princess with her face pressed against the familiar softness of the nursemaid.

"I go to live with my son in the Northlands. When you are older, you can come visit me. Won't that be fun?" The nursemaid spoke with forced cheerfulness through her tears. "But, come now, let me help you get ready for bed before I leave." Removing the gown, they folded it silently and placed it in the chest.

"Someday," said the nursemaid, "you will need to go to the wise woman of the fairies with this gown. She will know what must be done to restore its magic."

"I never want to wear it again as long as I live," said the princess shaking her head. "I don't want its magic."

"Someday you will feel differently," promised the nursemaid.

○   ○   ○

Personal Reflection

Dance in the Dark

✍ Parts of the parable that touched me are . . .

✍ When I read these parts I felt . . .

✍ Similar situations in my life are . . .

The princess in the story was violated. Whether we were sexually abused or not, many of us were hurt as children. Our treasure chests were opened and raided. Then the covers were slammed back down so no one would see our shame. We can reclaim our lost treasure only by opening the chest and looking at what's hidden in there.

We can affirm that we were hurt and were not responsible. Write the ways you were hurt as a child in the spaces around the treasure chest. Write how you thought, as a child, you caused the violation.

_____ hurt me by

(name)

_____

(name the incident)

As a child, I felt I caused it by

_____

(how I felt responsible)

But now I know it was not my fault. (Personal reflection for "Tears in the Light" will help you further in letting go of the self-blame)

_____ hurt me by

(name)

_____

(name the incident)

As a child, I felt I caused it by

_____

(how I felt responsible)

But now I know it was not my fault. (Personal reflection for "Tears in the Light" will help you further in letting go of the self-blame)

Support groups, counselors, and books can help us reclaim our own power and recover from childhood abuse. See Resources, page 177, for more information.

When the little princess grew to womanhood, her father arranged for her marriage to the son of a neighboring king to seal an alliance between their kingdoms. Although the princess grew to love the handsome and good-hearted prince, she dreaded their approaching wedding night.

On that evening, after the festivities, when the newlyweds retreated to their private chambers, the princess said with trembling in her voice, "My husband, if you would show your love to me, grant me this one request."

"Anything," answered the prince.

"Blow out the candles and close the windows so no moonlight enters. For I must be with you in the dark or not at all."

Thinking it the modest request of a new bride, the prince agreed. But, she requested it thus each night. Only after the darkness enveloped them would the princess put on her betrothal gown. She wondered how he could not know her anguish and wept silently as he touched her.

After many months of marriage, he began to push for light in their chambers at night. "I never tire of beholding you, my beloved. Let us leave the candles burning."

Each time she refused, but he continued to insist until one night after he slept she fled from the castle. The princess packed food, coins, and jewels for her journey along with the tattered betrothal gown so her shameful secret would not be discovered after her departure. Then she took the common clothes of a scullery boy to wear and left a gold coin in their place. In the still of the night, she led a swift horse from the stables and unlocked a back gate to slip out unseen. Her intention was to ride to the Northlands and find her nursemaid. She hoped the old woman was still alive, but if not, the princess would rather live unknown as a commoner somewhere than suffer the indignities of marriage.

Knowing that the prince would send out search parties with the morning discovery of her disappearance, the princess exchanged her well-bred horse for a sturdy old nag near dawn. The tinker sleeping soundly beside his wagon, would, no doubt, be pleased with the exchange. As for the princess, her disguise was now complete. In the daylight, knights from the castle thundered past the "servant boy" on the ponderous old horse in their hasty search to find the kidnapped princess. As she passed quietly through village after village, she heard the people talking about what might have become of her. Had trolls carried her off? Or, perhaps a dragon snatched her from her chambers.

The princess slept at night in the loft of stables and paid for food with common coins. After many day's travel she was glad to finally enter the Northlands and find the home of the nursemaid's son and his family. She was heartened to learn from him that his mother was well, but, alas, the woman had recently left for the land of the Great King. The princess accepted the son's offer for food and rest, all the while keeping up her servant boy charade.

The next day the princess once again set out, determined to be reunited with her nursemaid, even if it meant a long sojourn to the land of the Great King. The road there led into the wilderness. A great expanse of mountains and woods stretched out before her without any villages for comfort.

Her water skin was long empty when she stopped one afternoon at a murky pond. Massive trees crowded the embankment. Their gnarled roots winding down into the pool made it difficult for the princess to reach the water. The smell of rotting wood and stagnant leaves thickened the air, but she was thirsty. As she bent over to fill her water skin, a face appeared in the murky pond and she drew back, startled. It was her uncle beckoning her.

"Come be with me," he said. "I rule a kingdom now of uncommon beauty. See?" He waved behind him where cloudy skies were reflected in the water, even though the sky above the pond's trees was filled with sunlight. "I have found the mysteries of magic far greater than anything you have ever known. Come be with me. For you know that no one will ever love you as I do. You have nothing to hide or be ashamed of with me."

"No," whispered the princess as if in a nightmare.

He reached through the water and his hand gripped her arm, but it was not wet. "Come," he urged, pulling her toward the dark pool even as she cried out and struggled to free herself from his hold.

Suddenly, a blast of fire torched the pool, and her uncle disappeared in the ensuing steam. A horrible dragon, still snorting fire, descended from the sky into the pond, flapping webbed wings. The long neck snaked in and out of the water vigorously searching for some bauble, and then the horned, dripping head turned to the princess who was clamoring up the embankment to escape.

"I savor the day I will close my jaws around his despicable head," rumbled the dragon, who set down a great taloned paw to block the princess from leaving. The old horse had already bolted in terror and was nowhere in sight.

"Please do not devour me!" she begged. "You will not find much flesh on these bones. I would make a most unsatisfactory meal, I think."

"Do not be afraid. I wish to devour no one but the sorcerer or his trolls. You humans think we dragons are all alike. But, indeed, it was only a third of our kind who followed the evil dragon in his rebellion against the Great King. The rest of us do the King's business in far places and sometimes in these lands."

"Then you will let me go?" asked the princess with fear.

"No, I shall not. It is my duty to protect travelers who sojourn in the wilderness, for there are many dangers here. You cannot spend the night in these woods. I shall take you to the wise woman of the fairies. Her castle is a place of safety in the wild lands. From there, she can direct you on to the kingdom of the Great King."

With that, he took hold of her clothes in his daggerlike teeth and hoisted her onto his back. Sitting securely between the spiny projections, she watched in awe as the massive wings snapped twice and carried them into the air. They sailed high over the forest, but the trees grew taller and taller until they dwarfed the dragon. He lit in the branches of an oak so massive that a castle perched in the midst of its boughs.

"Welcome," greeted a pleasant woman standing at the open gate. Long, translucent wings pulsed gently behind her.

"I cannot stay, Wise Woman," apologized the dragon. "But, I have a visitor for you." The dazed princess was once again fetched in his mouth by the nape of her clothes and deposited at the gate. Then the metallic green creature launched into the air and was gone.

"Welcome, Princess," said the fairy woman who was neither young nor old, neither beautiful nor ugly, but when she smiled, the princess felt a wonderful peacefulness. They were nearly the same height, which caused the princess some bafflement.

"I thought fairies were all small," she exclaimed.

"We are, my dear. You wouldn't fit in the castle your own size, so we took the liberty of changing you to ours. But, do not be concerned. You will return to normal when you leave here." The woman led her into the castle, and the princess reached out a hand to steady herself against a wall as the ground rolled under her.

"I must be dizzy from the flight," she said.

"It is the wind. The castle sways in the branches of the oak. Most people grow to like it and say they never slept better than when they were rocked to sleep here by the breeze."

They entered a hall where a table full of food and drink awaited them, but no one else was in sight. "Refresh yourself," invited the woman.

"Where are your servants? Surely you do not live here alone," the princess asked curiously.

"Fairies have no need of servants. What we wish appears. And I have guests often who keep me company, but no others besides you at this time, although another will soon arrive."

"I have seen too many wonders today," the princess blinked and drank thirstily from the cup before her.

"So it is on any sojourn to the Great King."

"I do not go to see him, actually. It is my nursemaid I seek who is somewhere in his land. I could care less if I see the Great King since he is probably no different than any other man." She popped a grape into her mouth and was pleasantly surprised to find that it had no pit to discreetly discard.

"But, he's not really a man," said the wise woman warmly.

"Elf or whatever. Males are males, and I have no use for any of them."

"No, no," explained the wise woman gently. "He is neither human nor elf. Neither male nor female. Yet he is all of these."

"How can that be?"

"He is the Great King, and there is no other like him," answered the wise woman.

"But, doesn't he have many sons and daughters?"

"All adopted. Anyone who asks is adopted by him. Everyone in his kingdom is a prince or a princess."

"How very strange," puzzled the princess. But she was actually more interested in the food than the conversation. She had eaten only simple meals on her journey.

"There is no place I would rather be than in the court of the Great King," smiled the wise woman with a distant look on her face.

"Then why do you live here?" asked the princess, biting into a warm bread roll.

"Many are the sojourners who flee to this wilderness. Someone must live here to point the way to the King. Besides, once you have lived in his kingdom, it is never very far away. I am there often."

With that, the fairy woman glided unhurriedly through the air to hover at one of the hall's large windows. "Our next guest has arrived," she announced beckoning the princess to the window.

There outside in the outstretched branches below, the princess saw her husband climbing resolutely from bough to bough.

"Do not let him in!" cried the princess.

"I will not turn him away," answered the wise woman. "His journey has been arduous. And the higher he climbs in this tree, the smaller he becomes. The poor man is near exhaustion."

"Then, I beseech you, do not tell him I am here. It is from him I flee."

"I think not," said the wise woman cryptically as she slowly arched her arm into the air. The prince appeared miraculously in the hall, panting and bemused. Then his eyes fell on the princess, and he rushed toward her gladly.

"My beloved! You are alive! These many long weeks I feared you were dead!"

The princess thrust out a hand to stop his advance and reached with the other into the travel bag tied at her waist. Enraged, her only thought was to drive him away somehow. She intended to repulse him and thereby rid herself of his pursuit. Pulling out the tattered betrothal gown, she held it up for him in angry display.

His face fell and, momentarily, she felt a bittersweet victory. But she was not at all prepared for what came next.

He began to weep. She had never seen a man cry before. As his chest heaved, silent tears poured down his face. "My beloved, whoever has done this despicable thing to you, I swear will be slain. But do not fear that you would ever be loathsome to me. There is nothing that can keep me from loving you."

"Do not touch me!" she warned, stepping back as he came toward her once again. She was confused by the emotions bursting in her chest and the tears welling up in her own eyes.

"Only tell me who has done this and I will avenge you!" he asserted. "To steal you from my bed and violate you so hideously, surely this is a monster who merits the worst death. How thankful I am that you found sanctuary here with the wise woman. I will reward her tenfold for her saving kindness."

"No one abducted me," wept the princess fighting her tears. "I fled of my own accord because this has been the state of my betrothal gown ever since I was a child and my uncle danced with me." She threw the odious garment onto the floor.

The prince stared at her in disbelief before finding words to speak once again. "This does not change my love for you. It is your uncle I despise, not you."

"If you loved me, why did you add to the rips and stains of this garment? What I suffered with you was as disgusting as my uncle. You are no different. I only ask that you leave here and let me go my own way."

The prince's eyebrows pulled together in horrified apology. "Forgive me. I did not know . . . if I was clumsy or overeager, please forgive me. I did not know you were dissatisfied."

Taken aback by his remorse, the princess's anger abated slightly, but she still kept her distance from him.

The wise woman picked up the gown and turned toward the princess. "Many wicked spells from your uncle bind the magic in this gown, but it can be restored. Do you wish to have my help?"

"Why should I want this garment restored? In its untarnished state, its magic overpowered my uncle and caused him to dance with me."

"Ahh, that is one of his spells, to make you think the gown seduced him. But fairy magic doesn't work that way. It was your uncle's lust for power that brought him to your chambers. A sorcerer's magic is black because most of it is stolen from others. Indeed, after being banished, your uncle through sordid means has come to rule a dismal kingdom with many sorry inhabitants. He plans to conquer as many lands as possible to build himself an empire. Your uncle feasts on power like a vulture on flesh. That is what brought him to your chambers."

"Then this gown does not overpower men," said the princess, struggling to believe.

"You must tell me everything that happened with your uncle so that one by one we can discover and destroy the spells that have stolen the magic from your gown."

"It can truly be beautiful again?" asked the princess remembering how it had once glowed softly with magical color.

"Oh yes," answered the wise woman assuredly.

"And it is possible for me to enjoy wearing it with my husband?" she asked. The wise woman nodded again.

"Tell me where this uncle is, and I will slay him while you undo his dark magic!" blurted the prince.

"No," said the wise woman. "That is not for you to do."

"I will do whatever you require," pledged the prince to the wise woman, and he advanced as if to embrace his reluctant wife.

"Wait," the wise woman stopped him. "If you wish to help in the healing, you must not touch her until the spells are lifted and she invites your affection. Then, for a time, you must do only what she bids you until she is used to the magic."

"Surely there is some feat of courage or strength for me to perform in this restoration." The prince was disheartened.

"What I have asked of you will sorely test your strength and courage full well," said the wise woman kindly, and then she turned to the princess. "What is your decision? Do you wish to break your uncle's spells?"

The princess drew a deep breath, "Yes." She looked into the sincerity of her husband's face and felt a small stirring of her love for him.

○ ○ ○

Personal Reflection

Hope in the Wilderness

✍ Parts of the parable that touched me are . . .

✍ When I read these parts I felt . . .

✍ Similar situations in my life are . . .

The princess in this story hid in the darkness and finally fled in disguise into the wilderness. Many of us use disguises to hide our pain. Some of us try not to be attractive so no one will notice us like our abuser did. Some of us hide behind humor and happiness or act "cool," thinking no one will love us if they see our deeply wounded self. Some of us squelch our wit, intelligence, or energy, hoping we'll feel safer if we're invisible.

Make a mask (or masks) for yourself using paper bag(s) and markers or crayons to show the ways you hide your true self. Put on each mask and look at yourself in the mirror. Talk aloud to yourself about when you use this disguise and how it protects you. When you remove each mask, say aloud, "Now here's the real me." Smile at yourself.

You may want to journal about how this activity felt.

The princess fled into a wilderness. We all have our own emotional wilderness.

Who or what traps you in your wilderness?

✍ _____

_____

Who is your wise woman of the fairies? Who has helped you recover or grow as a person?

✍ _____

_____

What does a safe place where you can rest and heal look like?

✍ _____

_____

_____

TEARS IN THE LIGHT

○　　○　　○

The princess sat despondently in the sunlit window seat as she began yet another day recounting her uncle's evil deeds. The dingy betrothal gown in her lap was already wet from her tears. "Surely there is some other way to untangle these cursed spells," she said to the wise woman. "Remembering the dark nights of my childhood and speaking of them to you . . . I can no longer bear it."

"It is the only way to undo his evil," said the wise woman sympathetically.

"Can we not discard this gown and make a new one for me instead?" the princess asked through her tears with desperate hope.

The wise woman shook her head. "The magic in a betrothal gown can only be spun at the moment of your birth. This is the only one you will ever have."

"How could my uncle do such a wicked thing to me? I loved him so as a child," sobbed the princess with self-loathing. "How could I have been so foolish?"

"There! We have just found another one of his spells!" exclaimed the wise woman. "He wants you to blame yourself. We must break this the same as the others we have discovered over these past days. You must see the truth, embrace it, and speak it aloud."

With the tip of her finger, the wise woman traced the silvery outline of a circle that hung wondrously in midair. "We shall divide this circle of blame into pieces like cutting a pie. What portion belongs to your uncle?"

"Most of it, of course," answered the princess and directed the wise woman in drawing the segment.

"How much belongs to you?"

The princess pointed to the remainder of the circle, almost as much as she had assigned her uncle.

"Far too much," commented the wise woman. "What about your parents? Have they no part here?"

"For what?" asked the princess.

"Your father has some responsibility for what happened because he took no time for you, and so your uncle filled that void."

The princess's eyes filled anew with tears as she placed her own finger in the rim and drew a section of the circle for her father.

"And your mother, always so critical and chastising, she left you starved for your uncle's smiles," spoke the wise woman sadly. The princess slowly drew a section of responsibility for her mother.

"Your nursemaid, also," continued the fairy woman.

"No, no. Not my nursemaid. She alone loved me truly!" the princess protested.

"She failed to protect you even though she slept in the next room all those nights."

"She was hard of hearing," the princess defended her nursemaid vigorously. "It was not her fault. Once she suspected she watched for my uncle and then brought the guards to arrest him."

"Alright. Then let us assign part of the circle to her deafness, but not to her," offered the wise woman. The princess agreed. After these three additions, the portion of blame for the princess was now only a quarter of what it had been.

"It does not reflect the truth yet," the fairy commented with a flit of her wings.

"But what else could be changed?" asked the princess.

The wise woman pointed to the section of blame remaining for the princess. "This all belongs to your uncle. None of what happened is your fault."

"But I did what he asked!" the princess argued to prove her guilt.

"Children do what they are told. You were only a child. He was an adult and should never have asked you to make choices about your betrothal gown. He knew the meaning of what was happening; you did not."

"But, sometimes I asked my uncle to come to my chambers at night because I wanted to play hide and seek," the princess confessed with bitter shame.

"Even if you had asked him to dance with you, I would not blame you. If a child asked to play with a burning coal and the cook obligingly fetched one from the hearth, would you blame the child or the cook for the child's burns?"

"The cook, for the child didn't know any better, but the cook knew the coal would burn," said the princess slowly, and she felt as though an invisible weight had lifted from her shoulders. But then another self-accusation surged forward to replace what had been cast off. "Toward the end I knew better. I was old enough to know right from wrong."

"Like a troll training a griffin, your uncle wove his spells on you when you were very young. A full-grown griffin could easily break the metal troll-chain encircling its ankle. But, the trolls steal griffins as hatchlings from their mothers' nests and clamp a chain above one foot. The baby griffin pulls and strains, pecks and claws at the chain, all to no avail. After learning such helplessness, it gives up trying to escape. The full-grown griffin, in actuality, is chained by its childhood memories, not by the metal around its ankle."

The princess once again felt sadly relieved of a burden, but then another waiting self-accusation reared its head. "I kept silent. I should have told my nursemaid after it first happened because I knew she would stop it."

"Yes, but you also knew what would happen to your uncle. You protected him from harm at your own expense. Even when he was discovered, you pleaded for his life by taking blame on yourself. Such was the hold his spells had over you. You loved him with a child's selfless love, and he used that as a shield against discovery and punishment."

"If I am not to blame at all, then my uncle is even more evil than I realized," blurted the princess with newfound conviction.

"That is the truth," nodded the wise woman. "And it breaks this spell." As the silvery circle faded from sight, a hint of sparkle glistened momentarily in the betrothal gown.

So the days passed slowly in the fairy castle as the wise woman and princess unraveled the many cursed spells entangling the gown. The wise woman wept with her often as they discovered and dispelled the uncle's evil lies. While the dress became less tattered and stained, its magic glow had yet to return.

"Now that the spells are removed, you must do one last thing to restore the gown's magic. When you are ready, you must wash it in the forest pond that you fled from before coming here," explained the wise woman.

"But that pool is enchanted by my uncle. He nearly pulled me into his dark kingdom from it!"

"That is why you must return to the pool, to face him. His land is far away and he uses the pond, and others like it, as a looking glass to see where he wills. But this time you will be more powerful than he."

"What am I to say to him?" asked the princess with horror.

"The truth. Simply tell him the truth that you have discovered here, and he will not be able to harm you any longer. I will go with you, and, if you wish, you may invite your husband to accompany us."

"Yes. I think I would like him to come along," said the princess, thinking how she had grown to enjoy his company since he no longer touched her.

When the day came that the princess decided to sojourn to the pool, the wise woman called meadowlarks to fly them from the fairy castle. The flight on a soft feathered back was far more comfortable than the previous ride on rough dragon scales. The princess would have enjoyed the wondrous soaring through the air if not for her dread of the coming encounter. Once set down on the forest floor, she and the prince marveled at instantly returning to their normal size.

The wise woman flitted near them like a graceful hummingbird. "You must go down to the pond's edge alone while the prince and I remain here on the bank. Remember, you are more powerful now than your uncle."

Trembling, the princess climbed down the muddy, root-bound slope. The stench of wet, decaying leaves filled her lungs. She looked back for reassurance to where her companions stood waiting between the tall trees surrounding the pond. The prince met her eyes with worried concern. The wise woman of the fairies nodded to her with encouragement. Turning her gaze to search the murky depths of the water, the princess flinched when her uncle's face appeared there.

"I knew you would come to me again," he smiled warmly. "Our souls are bound together."

"What you did to me was wrong!" announced the princess fighting back tears. She had planned to be angry with him, but now felt only deep grief.

"Wrong? Is it wrong to love deeply and fully? There is nothing wrong with love," he said gently.

"There was nothing wrong with my love for you, but yours for me was not so pure. You stole the magic of my betrothal gown for yourself."

He smiled as if he were talking to an unreasonable child. "All the magic will be there as long as it is me you dance with. Come, be with me again. No one will ever love you as I do."

The sound of a sword unsheathing drew her attention to the embankment where her husband stood ready to charge if she but gave the word. The princess could hear the wise woman reminding him that this was not his battle.

To her uncle, the princess pronounced with more confidence than she actually felt, "You have no power over me any longer. I have broken the spells you cast on my gown."

His face fell, and he reached through the water toward her as if injured. But then the image faded away. The dirty pond became sparkling clear, and the muddy banks between the gnarled roots were now covered with soft, green moss. With joyful tears, the princess cast off the cloak that covered her gown and waded into the refreshing pool.

"I reclaim this gown for my own," she said aloud submerging herself in the water. Then she stood and looked down at the magical glow surrounding her. The betrothal gown, even though hanging wet on her, was dazzling in its delicate beauty.

The prince, waiting on the embankment, looked at her with wide-eyed wonder. She met his eyes willingly and moved toward him through the shallow water.

The wise woman of the fairies smiled and flew away unnoticed, leaving a glimmering trace of her presence along the path to the Great King's land.

○   ○   ○

Personal   Reflection

Tears in the Light

✐ Parts of the parable that touched me are . . .

✐ When I read these parts I felt . . .

✐ Similar situations in my life are . . .

Most people who were abused in any way as children—including sexual, physical, emotional abuse—tend to assume some of the responsibility for their own abuse. In the empty circle, assign the percentage of responsibility you give to yourself and others for abuse you have suffered. If there is more than one offender, draw additional circles. People you might assign blame to include the offender and people who might have protected you but didn't—parents, grandparents, teachers, God, yourself.

Assigning the Blame (including Blame I Feel)

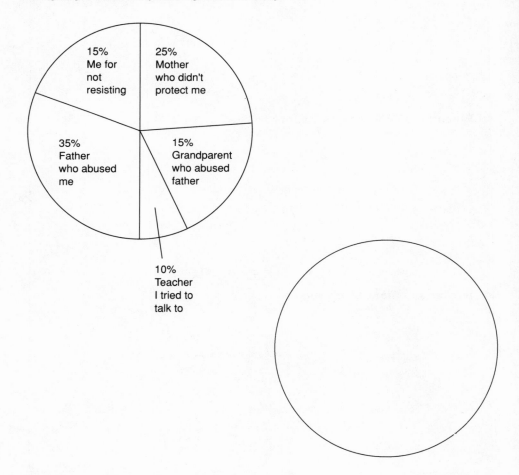

Reassigning the Blame

Now, redraw the chart assigning yourself no blame, even if you don't believe it yet. How does it feel to say "I was not responsible"?

Restoring Myself: The princess worked on her gown for a long time each day. In the space below, list some of the things you might do to restore your lost innocence. They might include daily meditation, self-affirmation, better eating habits, counseling, taking care of your physical or emotional needs in specific ways.

_____

_____

_____

_____

_____

_____

_____

On a separate sheet of paper, write a letter that you do not intend to send to the offender giving the blame back to that person. You may want to write about how you wrongly blamed yourself or how the incident affected your life. Claim your own power by telling how you are recovering.

SEA TIDE

o   EA   TIDE

o   o   o

The mermaid and her companions glided apprehensively through the dark, chilly water. No longer were these coast lands warmed and brightened by the sun. Since the sorcerer had come to the castle on the sea's edge, the sky was continually filled with blustery, cold clouds. The visibility underwater was so poor that merpeople had been ensnared by free floating nets that the sorcerer had released into the tides.

Surfacing to check her bearings, Miron sighted the lookout rocks where her triad would take the next watch. The mermen sitting there slapped their blue-green tail fins against the wet rocks in greeting when the new group bobbed up. Then Amrum extended a strong hand to help Miron slide onto the salty ledge.

"I had to sound the alarm twice during the night," he informed her and handed her the giant conch shell. "The sorcerer's trolls tried to harvest their nets for fish. We capsized two different rowboats and sent the trolls swimming for land. The sea serpents smashed the boats upon the rocks for us so they wouldn't float back to shore and be used again."

Amrum slipped into the sea with his companions and waved farewell.

"May your sojourn home be safe," said Miron before turning her eyes toward the shore. Dawn tinged the cloudy sky with dull pink. She could see dots of fires in the camp of the Great King. His army surrounded the sorcerer's jagged castle on land. At sea, her people and the giant sea serpents completed the siege circle and allowed no ships in to bring food or rescue to the sorcerer.

"It seems hunger would be more powerful than the sorcerer's magic," said Miron shaking her head. "Why do they refuse to surrender to the Great King? He asks nothing but that they pledge loyalty to him and leave off attacking neighboring lands."

"It makes no sense to me, Cousin," agreed Nusa, running her fingers through her seaweed hair as she settled into her spot on the lookout rocks.

"The sorcerer has vowed to die rather than bend his knee to the Great King," said Tro without taking his eyes off his assigned third of the sea. "I heard it yesterday from Esu who swims near shore often to take our news to the King."

The three passed the time talking, as good friends do, about the war, their loved ones, and secrets of the tides. To stay alert they sometimes sang ancient mersongs to the wind. As the tide came in, waves met the rocks and showered them with welcome spray, for the skin of a merperson must always stay wet. They no longer had to dive periodically into the sea to remain comfortable. Briny sea crabs skittered sideways across the rocks. Sea gulls circled noisily overhead following a school of fish. Some dolphins jumped playfully in and out of the surf. Fearing they might encounter one of the insidious nets, Miron watched protectively until the dolphins swam out of sight. Along the battlements of the sorcerer's castle she could see the movement of stocky trolls changing guard. Her watch would also be relieved soon.

At dusk, lights glimmered from the lowest windows of the castle, which sat half on land and half in water. Miron shuddered to think of what transpired in the grottos beneath the castle. Several mermen captured in the sorcerer's nets had been killed and eaten. But it was rumored that two mermaids were still alive, held prisoner to satisfy the sorcerer's dark desires.

She prayed the siege would soon end and put to rest forever the ominous evil that had engulfed her home waters.

Circular ripples in the ocean told her that the next watch was approaching. Nedra and her triad slid easily onto the rocks, which were half submerged by high tide now.

"May your watch be as peaceful as ours," said Miron, handing over the giant conch shell. Diving into the water, she gladly closed her lungs and breathed through her gills. Tro and Nusa swam eagerly ahead of her through the swaying seaweed. Though the day's light was fading, they would all be safely home before dark. At the corral reef they stopped to hurriedly eat a few clams and then continued on past the kelp beds toward the deep sea.

Suddenly, without warning, Miron felt a tug on her tail fin. Fearing the worst, she shimmied with all her strength to surge forward. Instead, she was snagged back, and the rest of the net closed around her. She pulled at the lattice of ropes, trying to find the edge to escape through. Tro and Nusa came instantly to her aid at great risk to themselves, for nets often capture more than one victim. While Nusa searched for the net's edge, Tro cut with all his might at the strands. But, the merman's sea knife and powerful muscles were of no avail against the magic cords.

"I'll find a sea serpent to free you," called Nusa as she swam away speedily. Only the sharp teeth of a sea serpent could cut through one of the sorcerer's accursed nets.

"Go with her," Miron demanded of Tro. "If she becomes ensnared alone no one would know where to find her. You know where I am."

"I will not leave you here alone!" protested the merman.

"You can help me more by going with Nusa and seeing that she safely finds a sea serpent. Now go before it is too late to catch up with her."

Tro nodded in agreement, his face filled with anguish. As he disappeared into the darkening water, Miron continued to struggle.

Her body become so tightly wrapped that her arms were bound over her head, and she could no longer even flip her tail fin. She twisted in the net as it drifted slowly toward the coral reef. If her friends did not return with help in time, it was quite possible that she would be battered to death on the shoals once the net caught in the surf. But she would prefer that to being hauled into a boat by trolls. Fighting panic, Miron realized that she could not even reach her knife to protect herself if she saw one of the sorcerer's boats approaching. She should have asked Tro to put it in her hand before he left.

"Miron!" the voice of a good friend called before anyone was visible.

"Over here," Miron cried out, and soon Ain was beside her.

"Do not struggle, my friend," pleaded Ain as she gripped Miron to stop her thrashing.

"Did they find a sea serpent?" Miron asked with hope.

"I don't know. But I met them on their way, and they told me where to find you. Listen to me, my friend. You must remain still. Although everything within you cries out to fight your way free, you must not do it, for that only entangles you more tightly in the net."

"What am I to do then?" Miron asked in desperation.

"Just float. Do not thrash or twist. Just float with the current until the net is loose around you. Then you can swim away free."

"I think you are addled, Ain," said Miron angrily as she began her fierce thrashing once again. "I remember when your grandmother told the same foolish story to our war council."

"No. Listen to me. My grandmother saw this work many times. She knew much about nets because the coast where she grew up was invaded by barbarians who had many fishing villages. The spell put on a net like this is clever: The more its prey struggles the tighter it becomes. Its source of strength is you. Be still and give it no power." Ain forcefully stopped Miron's twisting. "Please, friend, try what I'm saying."

Something in Ain's voice finally reached her, and Miron willed her body to be still.

"Good, good!" her friend encouraged her. "Now let yourself go limp." Miron hung helplessly in the net while panic surged in her soul.

"Now we must let time pass," Ain advised her. "Say these words to yourself: I am caught in a net, but it matters not. After a while I will float free."

Without movement, Miron gradually sank toward the ocean floor, and the net loosened although she was still thoroughly entangled. "Do not pull at the net," cautioned her friend. "Simply let it float away. Do nothing. Let the ocean currents tease it away."

Miron watched as miraculously an opening appeared in the net. "No, stay limp!" Ain warned as Miron raised her tail fin. "One flap of your tail, and the net will close in on you again."

So she waited. The minutes seemed unbearably long, but at last the net drifted away from her. She embraced Ain gladly in heartfelt thanks.

"How many other lives might have been saved if our people had believed your grandmother!"

"Solutions without might do not appeal to warriors," said Ain regretfully.

"Then we shall have to show them that this takes more might than any struggle," answered Miron resolutely as the two mermaids swam toward their home in the deep sea.

o   o   o

Personal Reflection

Sea Tide

✍ Parts of the parable that touched me are . . .

✍ When I read these parts I felt . . .

✍ Similar situations in my life are . . .

Naming My Stressors: Using the net diagram, list the stressors in your life and evaluate how you are handling them.

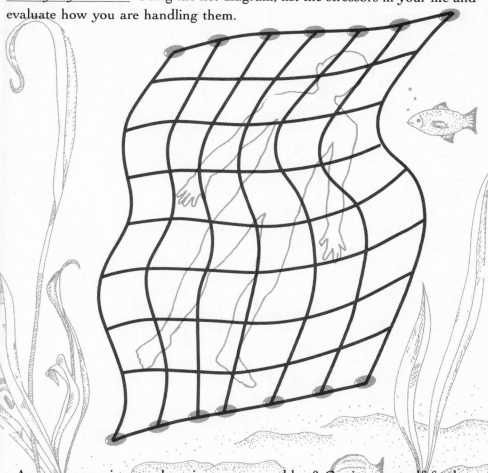

- Are you worrying or obsessing over a problem? Getting yourself further tangled in the net? Write a "w" for worrying beside that stressor.
- Are you denying you are stressed or have a problem? Are you refusing to implement a plan to rid yourself of the stress and staying tangled in the net? Write a "d" for denying by those stresses.
- Are you solving your problem by evaluating your situation, and implementing a plan to deal with it? As you implement the plan, you become untangled from the net bit by bit, day by day. Sometimes the plan may be just staying calm and serene so you don't become futher entangled, but can instead float out of the net. Write a "p" for plan by those stressors you're dealing with.

Stress Releasor: What parts of your body feel tense when you are anxious? Take a minute to feel them. To relax, start by tensing them even tighter, one at a time. Then let your body go limp as if you were floating in water. Do this whenever you realize you are anxious.

FESTIVAL OF
THE FOREST ELVES

o   o   o

*H*and *in hand, Avantar and Nalene wove their way through the*
merry crowd in search of Avantar's family. The moonlit grove overflowed with
the song and laughter of the elfin festival. Fireflies danced and twinkled in air
balmy with night blooming jasmine and honeysuckle.

From the canopy of trees overhead a voice called to them, and the young
couple smiled as they spied a good friend perched in the swaying branches.
"Lost in love or only lost?" teased Lamal.

"Both," answered Avantar.

"Let me be of most humble assistance to you. From my post here aloft
as lookout, I not only watch for trolls and all else evil that creeps at night, but
I can clearly see the location of your family, Avantar, over there." Lamal
pointed out the direction triumphantly. "And your family, fair Nalene, is at the
edge of the glen that way." He pointed again.

"Brave Lamal," said Nalene, "I'm so sorry you drew watch. We will miss
your company."

"The elders, no doubt, are glad to have you occupied," teased Avantar.
"For tonight they can be assured that no trek will ensue to do mischief in the
nearest village of humans."

Lamal grinned sideways. "And you, Avantar, were guilty of collusion on more than one of those boyhood treks. Remember the time we crept into the squire's manse while the household slept and stole the ledger where he recorded taxes owed by his overburdened villagers?"

"And the time we sewed some half-finished shoes for the cobbler, laughing as we imagined the amazement on his face when he sat down at his workbench the next morning?" Avantar reminisced. "We shrank ourselves as small as mice to get in and out under the door, and one of the cobbler's daughters woke to see us as we scrambled out."

"With such boyish pranks no wonder it is rumored among the humans that we are miniature." Nalene shook her head.

"Poor creatures, those humans. Did you know their eyesight is so bad they can only see clearly in the daylight? That is why they sleep all night instead of during the day like us," Lamal called down while scanning the perimeter of his area.

"Really?" Avantar commented with interest. What a dismal existence to live one's life in the sweaty heat and harsh glare of daylight. He preferred the gentleness of moon and starlight along with the soft glow that shone from within everything living, both plant and animal.

"Ho," Lamal called out, "Avantar, your family is beginning its opening dance. You'd best hurry."

Waving a hasty farewell, the couple headed off to find Avantar's kin gathered in a circle holding hands. They quickly joined the chain as the eldest matriarch of the family announced, "We celebrate life and all most dear: the love of our young who have married this year." She paused and the family members smiled toward Avantar and Nalene. "The beginning of new lives." Eyes turned warmly to an infant elf sleeping in a snug sling against its mother's heart and to a smiling cousin who was pregnant. "The memory of those who have enriched our hearts and gone before us into the beyond." The family gazed now into the past, thinking of those missed. "And great feats of skill or bravery known since the last festival will all be acknowledged. Let the dance begin!"

Breaking forth in jubilant song, the circle began to move swiftly, all feet in unison as leaves scattered. Even the youngest knew the steps.

Avantar watched Nalene throw back her head and laugh. Pale golden hair the color of a new harvest moon fell away from the curve of her pointed elfin ears. The rhythm of the dance guided them through the shared patterns, and Avantar willed his body to shrink as the whole group did so, without anyone missing a step. At their smallest size, the elves bounced atop the papery leaves of the forest floor as if on trampolines and laughed hysterically.

Keeping the circle intact was more of a challenge at this point, but still the family maintained itself by closing in tighter. Instead of hand in hand, they danced now with arms entwining waists and heads bent together. They were a tightly bundled orb swirling among the leaves and acorns. At the appointed moment in the song, they expanded once more to their full height. Suddenly Nalene broke free to dance by herself. With eyes closed, she was lost in the free-floating sensations of her movement. The sight of it caught Avantar's breath, not because of the beauty of her graceful dance (for it was wondrous to behold), but because this was not a thing done in his family. No one danced alone like this during the group songs. Aware of the shocked faces of his family, Avantar grabbed his bride by the arm to pull her back into the circle. Her eyes flew open in surprise and then momentary anger at Avantar, until she noticed the family was waiting on her to resume its dance.

The celebration continued without further embarrassment, and the incident was not discussed until much later as the two made their way through the crowded grove to join Nalene's family gathering.

"No doubt I shall be the talk of your relatives now for some time. What will they say about the poor misfit that Avantar married?" Nalene asked her husband irritably.

"No one would think more of it, if not for Aunt Gree who will bring it up in hushed tones to all she meets as if she pities you. My mother, no doubt, will defend you, saying that you have a good heart and cannot help your upbringing. And I shall laugh every time I remember the reddening of your face when you realized you had interrupted the dance."

"In my family it matters not if someone leaves the circle. The festivities would continue," Nalene bristled.

"In your family there barely is a circle," Avantar grinned but immediately regretted it when he saw Nalene's eyebrows pull together in fiery indignation.

"We don't celebrate like a clump of mushrooms. I can hardly breathe when *your* family closes in on itself in the tighter dances."

Avantar had no chance to defend himself because Nalene's relatives were now calling out greetings to the approaching couple. Obviously miffed, Nalene disappeared into the group and left Avantar to smile lamely at the kinfolk around him.

It seemed a disorganized gathering to Avantar with many songs and clusters of people dancing without touching. The small groups dispersed and rejoined in various combinations, and many elves split off to dance by themselves. Without the swaying movement from connected bodies, Avantar had to watch closely to keep up with the many changes in direction and pace of the circle he joined. Since they did not hold hands, members of the group intermittently shrank and expanded as the mood captured them. More than once, Avantar stumbled to avoid stepping on a miniature relative cavorting underfoot. At the last near miss, he nervously removed himself from the melee to stand at the side and simply watch.

"Feeling clumsy and awkward?" Nalene glided by, smiling smugly, and then danced around him in wide pirouettes. Avantar gazed at her in exasperation and wondered why a warrior such as he could battle mighty trolls but feel helpless in the face of his wife's wrath.

"Fair Lady," he sighed, "offer me terms for a truce, and let this enmity between us cease."

"No truce." She glided by again. "But, I will accept a surrender."

He was relieved to detect the hint of a smile at the edge of her lips. Dropping impishly to one knee, Avantar implored, "I am a cur most unworthy of my lady's favor."

Smiling as if reluctant, Nalene came to a standstill before him. Then, taking his arm to bid him rise, she kissed him long on the lips.

○　　　○　　　○

Personal Reflection

Festival of the Forest Elves

✐ Parts of the parable that touched me are . . .

✐ When I read these parts I felt . . .

✐ Similar situations in my life are . . .

Bridging the Differences and Getting Both Our Needs Met: Spouses or partners often find they come from very different families and have very different needs. This exercise may help you find ways to get both your needs met. It will also work for children, bosses, friends, and coworkers.

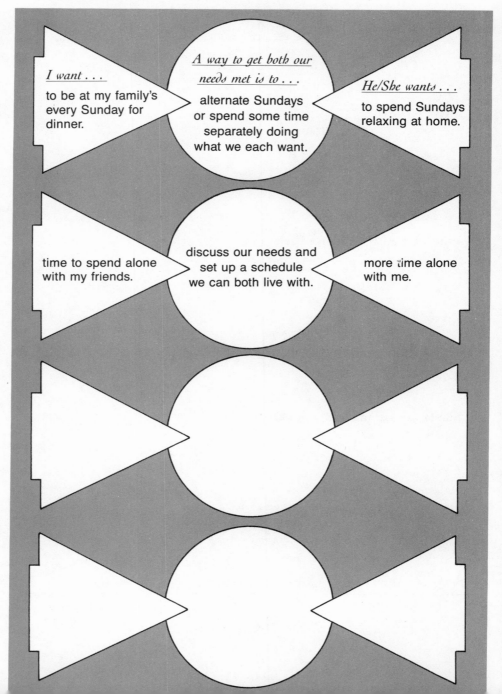

I want . . .
to be at my family's every Sunday for dinner.

A way to get both our needs met is to . . .
alternate Sundays or spend some time separately doing what we each want.

He/She wants . . .
to spend Sundays relaxing at home.

time to spend alone with my friends.

discuss our needs and set up a schedule we can both live with.

more time alone with me.

Draw a picture of the family you grew up in doing some activity that portrays the rules in their typical interactions.

What rules are you uncomfortable with? What new rules would you write for yourself?

✍ _____

_____

_____

_____

THE LONG JOURNEY

○   ○   ○

*T*he band of elfin warriors traveled at a swift pace along the moon-lit road. The call had gone out to join the Great King in battle, and so each clan had responded. From all the forests in all the scattered lands, hundreds of contingents made their way toward the King's encampment.

"The course I wanted to take through the valley would have been far less arduous than these mountain roads," Behar groused.

"Complain less and you'll have more breath for the journey," replied Lamal. He was tired of his cousin's constant harangue.

"You all agreed, better to traverse the mountains than travel the long way around," Behar raised his voice mockingly so that the rest of the band could hear him as well.

"Hush," reprimanded Lamal, speaking for all of them. "Do you want to alert every troll in the area of our presence?"

"There are fewer trolls in these mountains than the valley. Remember? That's why we came this way," Behar responded smugly.

"He may have the body of a warrior, but his insides did not grow with him," commented Nalene to her husband.

"Behar makes the journey long," agreed Avantar. "I have never seen Lamal so vexed. He is usually more jovial than all of us."

"I can't imagine why Behar's clan would think him fit for battle," remarked Myla, Avantar's sister.

"Perhaps they are hoping he will be killed," answered Nalene wryly.

Owls hooted indifferently from the trees as the band of elves passed by. Behar fenced along the road with an imaginary opponent and came up beside Myla.

"Do you prefer to slice trolls across the throat or up the gut?" he quizzed her.

"I slice trolls wherever I must to protect myself," answered Myla. In his mock battle, Behar whirled past Nalene and caught her foot with his. They both stumbled, but managed to right themselves.

"I'm sorry. It was an accident, I swear it," Behar pleaded into her indignant face, but she sensed he was stifling a sneer.

"Do not walk near me," Nalene threatened Behar in a low voice. "Stay your distance." She took the lead in the band, but glanced back periodically to check the whereabouts of the troublemaker.

As the night drew to an end, the elves left the road to search out a safe place to sleep during the day. They gathered a few mushrooms and acorns to eat, and then spotted a tree with several hollow knotholes.

"Perfect," pronounced Avantar straddling a tree branch and peering in the nearest knothole. He reached in and scooped out the old leaves caught there. Then Nalene handed him a clump of soft, fresh greenery. He always let her pick the bedding, for she was more sensitive to smells than he. She climbed up in the tree beside him, and then they both shrank to a size comfortable for the hole before crawling inside. In the knothole above they could hear Myla already snoring. Somewhere lower in the tree they heard the muted voices of Lamal and Behar arguing.

"I hope Lamal can talk some sense into him," said Avantar plumping leaves to form a pillow.

"He won't listen," Nalene pulled a wide green leaf over them. "Someone like Behar thinks of no one but himself. He will continue with his antics, and we will have to leave him behind at the next glen of elves we come to."

"He won't stay there," Avantar's eyebrows lowered in concern. "And he might be set upon by trolls if he follows after us alone."

"That would not be our fault if he made such an imprudent choice. I would be sorry to hear of it. But I would prefer he suffer alone for his folly rather than bring a brace of trolls down on us," challenged Nalene. "His foolishness endangers us all. He is simply not a safe traveling companion. It is time to leave him behind."

"That still seems vengeful," Avantar sighed.

"If we were vengeful we would set upon him ourselves. Or lay in wait and harass him as he has us," Nalene explained, slightly irritated at her husband's softheartedness.

"So then, what place has forgiveness in all of this?" asked Avantar, still bothered.

"If Behar saw the problem of his behavior and promised to stop endangering us, I would be willing to forgive him. I'd give him another chance. But, he's not the least bit sorry for what he's done. He apologizes to placate us, not because he intends to change. That, to me, is not a sincere apology."

"He clearly has no intention of changing his ways," agreed Avantar.

"I tire of Behar. Enough about him," said Nalene with her head propped up on one arm as her other hand caressed Avantar's chest. He reached for her gladly, but suddenly she threw herself over him with her sword raised. He rolled out of the way as a hairy spider fell dead upon their bed. Nalene withdrew her blade from the creature's abdomen and its prickly legs spasmed one last time. The carcass covered the bed of leaves.

"I hate spiders," said Nalene.

They ate their meal of nuts and mushrooms in the twilight as they traveled once more. The forest grew thick around them with branches overhanging the road above their heads. Myla felt something small hit her head and suspiciously scanned the canopy above her. Smaller dragons sometimes perched hidden in treetops waiting for unwary prey to happen by. But alert travelers would notice the falling acorns disturbed by a dragon's meandering tail. Again she felt the slight impact against her head and searched the branches overhead.

"Behar, stop it." Nalene halted the band. "You are throwing pebbles at Myla. Do not deny it."

"Nalene, really, are you jealous that I am flirting with Myla?" Behar teased. "If you were not already taken, I swear I would have thrown the pebbles at you as well."

"How are we to be alert for trolls or dragons with such foolery from you?" demanded Lamal.

"Are we to have no fun on this journey? You are humorless warriors indeed!" Behar defended himself.

"No, you are the humorless one," Lamal said pointing an accusing finger at his cousin. "I've told you more than once, this pestering will stop, or we will leave off traveling with you. I will not have you endangering our lives."

"Any troll so stupid as to attack us will be easy enough to dispatch. They might be brawny, but their brains are smaller than a—" Behar's bravado suddenly faded, and his face blanched with genuine fear. "Did you hear that? Something's in the woods."

The band of elves apprehensively drew their swords and paired back to back scanning the forest on both sides of the road. The tense silence was broken by a burst of laughter from Behar who could no longer control himself.

Nalene swung to face him angrily, her sword still in hand. "A warrior never jokes about such matters."

Behar's face sobered, "I'm sorry. I thought it would be a good laugh for everyone." His pointed elfin ears twitched with discomfort as he faced four very angry companions.

"The thought of trolls is never funny," said Avantar sheathing his sword.

"You will stay behind in the next elf glen we reach," Lamal stated firmly.

"Come now," protested Behar. "I said I was sorry."

"You're sorry we're angry at you, but you have no intention of stopping your behavior, do you?" Nalene inquired testily.

"What kind of friends are you?" exclaimed Behar. "Can't you enjoy a little jesting now and then?"

"I fear you are the one who has much to learn about friendship." Avantar shook his head sadly.

"You will stay behind in the next elf glen we reach," Lamal repeated adamantly.

"I'd like to see you try and make me," guffawed Behar.

"That you shall," promised Lamal resolutely.

Not much further on their journey, they came to a glen inhabited by elves. No sooner had they been welcomed, than Lamal apologetically brought the dilemma about Behar to the council of elders.

"My cousin exaggerates," complained Behar. "He and his friends are overly fearful of trolls and would have me creep about as quietly as a mouse on this journey. That is no way for a warrior to travel!"

"Tell me Behar, how many trolls have you fought in your lifetime?" asked one gray-bearded elder.

"A score to be sure," boasted Behar.

"I greatly doubt that," said the elder. "If you had ever fought for your life even against one troll, you would be cautious about meeting another."

The other elders nodded in agreement. "You will stay here until your friends return," pronounced the matriarch for the council.

As the band of warriors thanked the elders and departed, they heard Behar's fierce protests, muffled from a huge barrel, his temporary prison.

o   o   o

P e r s o n a l   R e f l e c t i o n

The Long Journey

✍ Parts of the parable that touched me are . . .

✍ When I read these parts I felt . . .

✍ Similar situations in my life are . . .

Who has been a Behar—someone who was unsafe for you to be around—in your life?

✍ _____

How did you decide whether it was possible to forgive and reconcile or time to let go and take separate paths?

✍ _____

_____

Is there any relationship you need to let go of? Perhaps you have given this person too many chances without ever receiving a sincere apology or amends.

✍ _____

Is there anyone who has made genuine attempts at reconciliation that you need to forgive?

✍ _____

Is there a time or relationship in your life when you were Behar? What would you like to do about that?

✍ _____

_____

_____

We're each responsible for our own recovery. We can only change our own behavior, not that of others. Attending a Twelve-Step group or working with a Twelve-Step book can help us remember that. See Resources, page 177, for a listing of groups and books.

BATTLE BOG

o   o   o

*T*wilight deepened as the elfin warriors prepared to leave their encampment and take up their positions on the siege line encircling the enemy. In the distance lay the sorcerer's castle, starkly outlined against the dark gray of the continually cloudy sky. Driven from his conquered lands in battle after battle by the Great King's forces, the sorcerer now sat entrenched in this last refuge on the sea. Off shore, the merpeople and sea serpents loyal to the Great King capsized or blocked supply and rescue ships from reaching the castle. Vicious bands of the sorcerer's troll army were now creeping from the fortress, not to break through the siege line, but to attack and eat any of the King's soldiers they might overpower. Some trolls had surrendered out of fear that stronger trolls would devour them within the castle. They had seen others perish so. Still, the sorcerer would not surrender. So great was his arrogance; he had vowed to die rather than bow his knee to the Great King.

Avantar watched as Nalene resolutely sharpened her sword, smoothing out the nick her blade had taken when it met a troll's thick axe the night before in battle.

"Sometimes I doubt I have the heart of a warrior," Avantar confessed as he buckled on his own sword with dread for the coming night. "I would much rather be back home dancing with you in the festival grove."

"Noble warriors do not enjoy battle. We do what we must." Nalene ran a finger gingerly along her sword blade. Then, satisfied with its condition, she sheathed it. "If you relished the blood of war, I would not have married you."

"Who would you have married?" Avantar embraced her, smiling despite his heavy heart.

"Maybe Palincsar."

"Palincsar?" Avantar protested as if injured.

"Even though he doesn't have your amber wolf eyes." Nalene gently stroked the side of Avantar's face. Their exchange of kisses was interrupted by someone throwing clumps of moss at them.

"Have you no shame?" teased Lamal as he launched another moss wad.

They walked together with Lamal and Myla toward the boglands where a legion of nocturnal elves would relieve the humans who had held the siege line during the day. Haggard human soldiers, some wounded, passed them on the way.

"If they would only let their women fight alongside them, perhaps they would have fewer casualties," Nalene commented with concern.

"Human women aren't strong enough to wield swords," Lamal explained.

"Do not believe it," asserted Nalane. "Someone has only made them think they're weak. One of the sorcerer's tricks most likely."

They took their positions, crouched behind a bulwark built of mud and clumps of swamp grass. Avantar's knees sank into spongy, wet ground as he scanned the bogland stretching out before him for any sign of movement. Like all elves, his night vision allowed him to see the soft glow of living plants and creatures. Knowing this, the trolls had been wrapping themselves with skins of dead animals to hide their dim outlines while crawling through the swamp with only their eyes exposed. So Avantar watched for the faint glow of eyes or the movement of uprooted plants being used as screens. He sifted the air coming in his nostrils to find any scent of troll among the acrid, dank odors of the marsh. His ears took in every sound that broke the morose litany of crickets and frogs: the calls of nightbirds, the lapping of the tidewater filling the marsh, the splash of a fish escaping from a water snake, the rustling of leaves and reeds when a breeze arose.

The depth of the cricket cadence abruptly shifted. Some chorus members had become silent. Avantar and Nalene exchanged knowing glances and felt the tension rise among the elves lining the long bulwark.

Dark shapes suddenly stood from the black water and charged from behind reeds. All along the siege line the sound of metal meeting metal clanged. Hoarse troll roars filled the air.

Avantar raised his sword to block the downswing from a wide troll blade. Although the force of it jarred his entire body, he simultaneously kicked the stocky attacker in the stomach. The troll sneered and swung his heavy axe at Avantar again, but the elf dodged it and swiftly shrank to the size of a mouse. What had been ankle-deep water, was now a lake for Avantar to swim in between the gigantic legs of the cursing troll. The attacker pivoted to search for his quarry and stomped randomly in hopes of crushing the elusive elf underfoot. The turmoil of waves created by this carried Avantar behind the troll where he expertly expanded to his full height, equal to his enemy, and sank his blade into the troll's side. The wound was not mortal, and the struggle continued until four more hardwon slashes felled the hateful creature.

The battle raged with another surge of trolls replacing those slain before them. Avantar and Nalene fought back to back to guard each other from assault, for the fighting was thick now with trolls and elves on every side. Unfortunate elves who fell under the axes, even if still alive, were torn limb from limb and devoured by their attackers. Some were carried off into the marsh. As they fought, the area became strewn with corpses of trolls and, as was usual, Nalene felled as many as Avantar.

Out of the corner of his eye Avantar saw Nalene stumble. He turned from his own attacker to defend her, but she was not there and, assuming she had shrunk to protect herself, he faced his enemy again. Beyond that hulking form he saw a troll retreating into the swamp with Nalene slung limply over its shoulder. Horrified, Avantar charged past his opponent to go after her, but was jerked back by a vicelike grip on his arm. He swung about and heaved a blow at the assailant, but was shocked to find his blade meeting Lamal's upraised sword. It was Lamal who gripped his arm.

"Let go of me! Nalene's been taken!" Avantar twisted free but was thrown to the ground when Lamal leapt on him and pinned him down.

"She's dead! You can't help her!" Lamal's face was contorted as he wrestled with his friend. Above them, Myla moved in to stand guard over the struggling pair and fend off trolls.

Enraged, Avantar brought his knee up to knock Lamal off. "She will be dead if you hold me back!"

"She's already dead! I saw the blow that took her head off! She was dead before the troll carried her off. I'm sorry, Avantar. She's dead." The desperation in Lamal's eyes brought panic to Avantar.

"No."

"Would I restrain you if there was any chance she was alive? I would be the first by your side to go after her."

Not wanting to believe Lamal's words, Avantar renewed his struggle for release. He would go after her even if he had to kill Lamal. Two more elves were suddenly on top of him. Avantar felt enraged when these friends, too, ignored his pleas. Despite his thrashing, they dragged him back to the place where he had fought most of the night.

Lamal stooped among the troll bodies and said, "I'm sorry, Avantar." There at Lamal's feet lay Nalene's head.

The truth tore at Avantar with pain so great it crushed his chest. A wail escaped his lips that would have annihilated all life if it were within Avantar's power. Without Nalene, there was no reason for the world to continue.

Avantar sat in his tent staring at nothing in particular. Soft daylight filtered in and fell on Nalene's empty bedding. It was the middle of the day. Because elves are nocturnal creatures, the entire camp was quiet with sleep.

Lamal and Myla had stayed awake with Avantar until they could no longer hold their eyes open and now lay slumbering on one side of the tent. Snatches of conversations from the past few days repeated themselves hollowly in Avantar's head.

"She would still be alive if I were a better warrior," his own voice accused.

"You know that's not true," Lamal had challenged. "We were overrun by them, and many kindred were lost."

"She has gone beyond where there is no pain or need," another friend said—words that would have angered him if not for the tears in her eyes. She had loved Nalene like a sister.

"Why was she taken instead of me?" Avantar agonized and felt guilty for resenting that those gathered around him were alive instead of Nalene.

"At least she wasn't eaten alive." One of the youngest warriors had attempted to offer comfort but received stern glances from the others instead.

"It was a clean blow that took her. She went quickly."

"We will all miss her greatly."

"I'm so sorry."

"She was so strong and full of life."

"She loved you with all her heart."

"Chiuld, Garn, and Baye are gone as well." The loss of these friends added to a grief already overwhelming.

"Lotar and Eglund are sorely wounded and not expected to live."

"Havgan lost an arm. Norn's eye was put out."

The elves buried their dead in a large funeral mound with many testimonies to the honor and bravery of the deceased warriors. The ceremony seemed to Avantar both interminably long and far too short. Eulogies could not capture even a small fraction of the fullness of the lives lost.

There were embraces and tears but, finally, only Lamal and Myla remained to sit silently with Avantar.

In the days that followed, Avantar knew both helpless desolation and powerful rage. They lived within him like beasts struggling for predominance. He avoided people and kept to himself because he did not wish to talk about Nalene's death. At the same time, there was nothing else to speak of. The thought of telling someone who had not heard shriveled his very being. He could not bring himself to say the words aloud.

He was tortured by anger at himself and ruminated over countless ways he might have kept her from harm. "If only I had . . ." His friends allowed him to return to the siege line the following nights only after he vowed to them that he would not willingly give up his life to a troll's axe. He assured them he was committed to avenging Nalene's death by slaying every troll that came across his path. And so he did with a thirsty vengeance.

But his most wrenching anger was at the Great King, for it was unspeakable. Avantar imagined the horrified faces of the other elves if he were to say his thoughts.

"Why are we here? Isn't it true that the Great King could have destroyed the sorcerer long ago? Why does he let this siege drag on? Would a King who really cared about his people allow such carnage?"

Many were the hours Avantar had spent in the King's presence. Now he thought himself a fool for being so loyal. Avantar no longer fought for the King and his cause, whatever that was. He fought only because there was a perverse satisfaction of sorts whenever he eviscerated another troll. But the satisfaction was all too brief. After each battle, emptiness and desolation clutched cold fingers around his soul once more.

He fought back by fantasizing about storming the castle and throwing the sorcerer to his death from the battlement walls onto the rocky shore of the sea far below. But even at the end of this siege Nalene would still be lost to him.

Only the Great King, who knew the oldest and deepest magic of the land, could bring her back. Very few were those who had returned from beyond. Still, it was Avantar's only hope.

The King's tents were pitched between the human and elfin encampments. Avantar stood outside for some time with the salty night air blowing against his face and watched the movement of people inside the illuminated tents. Resolved to gain his request at any cost, he entered and asked an attendant for a private audience with the King.

He was ushered in without a wait and, seeing the King's face, he steeled himself for his mission.

"Avantar," the King greeted him sadly. "This siege has been far too costly, has it not?"

"Yes, far too costly."

"I am glad you have come."

Avantar found that surprising.

"We have much to talk of," the King continued and bid him to sit.

"You have it within your power to bring her back," blurted Avantar, declining the seat. "Ask whatever you wish of me, and I will do it. If there is any service I have resisted, any task from which others shrink in fear . . . only promise me Nalene, and I will obey any command you issue."

The King winced. "I have never taken slaves, Avantar. My subjects are all free persons. And any gifts I bestow are given freely."

"Then I beg you to bring her back from the beyond, for it was not right that her life ended so prematurely."

"It is true that Nalene should have lived a long life with you if not for the sorcerer's evil. But now that she is gone, it is best to leave things as they are."

"Then send me to the beyond as well, for I despair of life here." Infuriated by the callousness of the denial, Avantar seized from the tent's wall the royal sword where it hung sheathed and threw it to the King. Then, pulling his own weapon, he charged, intending to force the sovereign to slay him in self-defense. But the King deliberately dropped the royal saber on the ground and stood waiting for Avantar's attack.

Incensed, Avantar swung his sword with all his might. It should have cut half way through a torso, but the King caught the blade across the palm of his hand, and grasping it as the blood dripped to his wrist, he wrenched the sword forward until Avantar fell against him. He held Avantar tightly against his chest even as the warrior flailed and struck him. Finally, Avantar's rage broke forth in angry tears as the desolation swept over him. He sobbed like a child in the Great King's arms.

It felt as though he would drown in the hemorrhage of emotion. The pain was a black and endless roiling sea. After unmerciful aeons he found himself exhausted and washed onto a barren shore. Collecting himself, he pulled away from the King in weary embarrassment.

"Forgive me." He stared at the caked blood on the King's hand. "I am a most unworthy warrior."

"There is no dishonor in grief. It is the most difficult of all journeys, with many fierce battles along the way. All are brave who embark on the path of mourning."

"I did not choose this road."

"No one does. But many think they avoid the pain by balking at the head of the path. In truth, they only prolong their suffering."

"What reason is there to sojourn? Will I find along the way some salve to mend my anguish?"

"No ointment is strong enough for a wound as deep as yours," the King answered with sorrow. "You will find healing only by following the pain to its finish. There is no other way."

"Then there is no healing, for my love for Nalene will never be finished. I will not embrace solace if it banishes her from my memory."

"Be assured, you will never stop loving her. But, with time, your memories of Nalene will bring pleasure instead of pain."

So they sat, talking through the night until dawn tinged the cloud-covered sky with pink and gold. In the morning light, shadows clung to the sorcerer's bleak castle as elfin and human warriors exchanged vigils on the siege line of the bog.

○   ○   ○

Personal Reflection

Battle Bog

✍ Parts of the parable that touched me are . . .

✍ When I read these parts I felt . . .

✍ Similar situations in my life are . . .

Naming Our Losses: Grief is a process. We can't grieve something we're not willing to admit we've lost. Use the space below to list some of your losses. They may include death of a loved one, loss of a job, loss of a marriage, loss of a happy childhood, loss of respect of others.

After each loss, write how you felt about it when you first realized it. In the third column, write how you feel about the loss now. If you don't feel resolution, what can you do to acknowledge your feelings so that eventually you can go on with your life? It hurts to grieve. But it hurts worse not to grieve because you either cut off your ability to feel anything or stay stuck in anger, bargaining, and depression.

My Losses	*How I Felt about My Loss When It Happened*	*How I Feel about My Loss Now*

In grieving, more than any other time, we struggle with questions about whether our Higher Power cares or exists. Like Avantar, we might attack God because of our pain and desperate rage. God is strong enough to take our anger. The Great King held Avantar until the warrior no longer struck him but could cry in his arms. In this space, let your Higher Power know how you feel.

I feel so angry at you because . . .

✍

I wish you had . . .

✍

I hurt so bad when I think of . . .

✍

There are many books to help cope with the pain of loss and grieving. See Resources, page 177, for more information.

THE CURSE

o   o   o

"My King, why do you not storm the castle and end this? The siege drags on far too long," Sir Weyd, high captain of the army, spoke with exasperation in the privacy of the Great King's field tent.

"From the beginning of the campaign I have announced my goal to see Chastain's surrender not his death," said the Great King, reaffirming his position. Sir Weyd noted an unusual heaviness of heart in the King's voice.

"I have no use for Chastain. I would run him through without a moment's hesitation. And glad will be the day when every last troll is dead," Sir Weyd said fervently.

The King smiled slowly and knowingly. "Your hate is not as deep as your words, Weyd. Just last week you found an abandoned infant troll in the marsh. You could not bring yourself to slit the orphan's throat and took it to be tended by the troll women in the prisoner's camp."

Weyd reddened as the King continued. "Even trolls can learn to live in peace. Look at how many have come to us, thankful to find a safe haven from Chastain's rule. One day the rest will join us as allies."

Weyd exhaled in exasperated doubt. "I cannot picture such a thing and certainly not a sorcerer like Chastain as a loyal subject. He has vowed to die before bowing his knee to you!"

"It will come, but not easily," said the King with such a weighted soul that Weyd searched his face with concern.

"Remember, my friend," said the King looking deeply into Weyd's eyes, "no matter how dark matters seem in the coming days, do not give up hope."

As he had done on many occasions, Sir Weyd accompanied the King by horseback to the siege line where they stopped within shouting distance of the blighted castle. Chastain, the sorcerer, stood waiting on the battlements surrounded by his hunkering trolls. The sorcerer's fiery charisma was apparent in the carriage of his lean body and in the regal tilt of his head as he threw taunts to the King.

"Will you end the siege today, Great King? That is what your armies cry out for. They lick their lips imagining the taste of my death and think that would give them victory. But you and I know the truth. My death will end no strife, not really. The power of the dragon fills the air; all of you have breathed in the spores of his breath. Even before you left your land, your people at home and this very army were infected, Great King, with a disease that no physician can heal. If you kill me, someone else will rise up to take my place in leading the rebellion against you. Perhaps it will even be one of your most trusted knights. Maybe Sir Weyd or Sir Brin will turn against you and seek the dragon's succor. In the end, no one will be able to remain loyal to you. No matter how steadfast their intention, they will succumb."

Unable to contain himself, Sir Weyd lifted his sword angrily toward the sorcerer. "Your arrogance is only outmatched by your lies, Chastain! Would you further test the King's mercy, which he has extended despite your unworthiness? Command your army to lay down their arms and surrender yourself to the King before his grace is withdrawn."

Chastain's mouth stretched into a straight, thin-lipped smirk. "You are a fool, Weyd. Mighty as you are, you could rule ten kingdoms, yet you serve the King. Would you not have handled this whole campaign better from the start? Would you not have been more thorough than the Great King in slaughtering my troops and cutting us off so we would never have reached this stronghold? Even now you chafe at the bit the King has placed in your mouth to hold you back from charging these walls. Why do you follow him when his ways no longer make sense to you?"

"How long will you allow this perverse railing to continue, my Lord?" Weyd turned to the King. "His tongue twists truth and lies together like a rope to hang us. Give the order and let me silence him forever!"

As a parent would calmly hush a child, the King held up a hand to bid Sir Weyd to quit.

"You may win this siege, mighty King," Chastain called out. "But you cannot win in the very end. The dragon will prevail because to serve him is to serve ourselves."

"Chastain," the King, sitting upon his restless charger, called up to the sorcerer. "Let us see whose magic is stronger, yours or mine. Let the two of us meet alone, face to face."

"Do you think me a fool to bait me with such a ploy? I will not be lured outside these walls. No matter what your command, your motley horde would not stay back if I set foot outside this castle. They would even trample you, their King, underfoot in their rush to slay me."

"If you will not trust me to meet outside the gate," said the King, "then allow me to come to you inside the castle."

"My Lord, no!" exclaimed Sir Weyd accompanied by an uproar from the King's troops. Once again, the King held up his hand for silence.

On the battlement wall, Chastain's face was quizzical but pleased. "If the Great King wishes to visit me within my walls, who am I to deny him that privilege?"

"Sire, you cannot mean to do this!" implored Sir Weyd.

"I will return to you in a few days' time," answered the King. "Until then continue the siege. Do not storm the castle."

"You cannot go in there! It is a thing without reason or sense!" The high captain was beside himself.

"That which holds the greatest power does not always seem sensible," said the King breathing out.

Sir Weyd fully intended to physically restrain him, but found he was unable to move as the Great King rode slowly toward the lowered drawbridge of the castle. Weyd watched with horror as the King entered the gates and the heavy, latticed iron thudded loudly to close the King from view. Only then was Sir Weyd released from whatever had held him immobile.

Agitated and confused, the King's army waited tensely through the day. The elves took their shift at nightfall similarly overwrought, for they had been awakened earlier with the disconcerting news about the King.

Also at nightfall the dragon arrived, swooping over the siege line to perch upon a tower of the castle. A great din of raucous trolls could be heard from within the fortress. Bonfires in the courtyard cast flickering orange light onto the belly, chin, and snaking neck of the dragon, who attentively watched what transpired beneath him. Periodically, the dragon flapped his wings and roared with delight as flames shot from his nostrils.

Sir Weyd and his captains agonized over whether to wait as they had been instructed. Would the King's safety be endangered or ensured by storming the castle? At dawn Sir Weyd issued the order to attack.

Unleashed after so many long months of restraint, the King's army swiftly annihilated the trolls guarding the outer battlements. Chastain's forces were clearly not expecting an attack. The King's soldiers who scaled the walls opened the gates and lowered the drawbridge for the waiting army to enter. They were met by an onslaught of trolls pouring out of their quarters.

The fighting became fierce and was no longer the rout Sir Weyd had hoped for after the initial success. The death toll on both sides climbed. All the while, the dragon perched on the lofty east tower and watched the battle with haughty amusement. Strangely, Chastain made no appearance to taunt the attackers or stir his own forces to a frenzy. Neither had the King come before them. Something was amiss in the castle. Though Sir Weyd could not determine what it was, he knew in his soul that something was terribly wrong.

The bleak castle had four separate walled courtyards within it, and each had to be taken for the fortress to fall. Late in the night, Sir Weyd and his finest knights, hacking and slashing, finally broke through the troll defense to scale the walls around the east courtyard. They entered warily with an eye on the dragon who sat quietly upon the tower as if gloating.

Inside the courtyard, the horror that met Sir Weyd's eyes was more than he could bear. The knights stood beside him, momentarily pausing in stunned silence.

The Great King was chained to the fortress wall where he had been beaten and tortured. Fighting back tears of rage and pain, Sir Weyd strode forward and smote the chains to free his King. Flies disturbed by the activity rose from the body and hovered in the night air around the knights as they carefully laid the King on the ground.

"We must cover him with our cloaks to warm him," commanded Sir Weyd as he removed his own.

"There is no way to warm a corpse." Sir Brin, second in command, gripped the captain's shoulder. With those words Weyd faced the obvious and let the hot tears push through.

Above the din of battle around them, the dragon's smug voice rumbled loud and low, "We had great sport killing him last night while you did nothing. You are fools, as was your King!" Swooping from the tower the dragon batted at them with his treacherous claws like a cat toying with trapped mice.

"Take the King into that tower," Sir Weyd instructed his men while he grabbed hold of a scaling rope and the multi-hooked prong attached to it. Swinging it with all his hate and might he met the dragon's next swoop. The prongs caught and tore along the sinewy edge of one wing. The dragon roared flames toward his assailant, but Sir Weyd quickly rolled into the protection of the tower and escaped harm.

"I will slay that creature or die trying," vowed Sir Weyd out loud to the stiff and disfigured body of the King. He knew his troops would be spurred the same by the news spreading of the King's treacherous murder.

"Captain," one of his men urgently approached him. "They've found Chastain on the next floor." With his knights following, Weyd bounded up the circular stone stairs.

"He is still alive, Sir," the elfin warrior informed him as he kneeled over Chastain. "We found him this way; laying here fallen as if in a swoon."

"He is, no doubt, in some dark trance, lending his power to the defense of this castle. Give me the honor of cutting his throat, and I will give you all my wealth," begged Sir Brin passionately.

"No," Sir Weyd stared at the hated sorcerer's unconscious face. "We shall execute him slowly at dawn on the battlements in full view of where the fighting continues. We shall draw and quarter him and throw pieces of his body out to his cursed trolls to dishearten them and rally our own troops."

"But, the dragon—" Sir Brin's concern was interrupted by his commander.

"—we will contend with the dragon as we carry out the execution. If he hopes to rescue Chastain from us, he will have to limit his fire, for that would roast Chastain as well. So we shall only have to worry about his jaws and talons. That we can do battle with."

Through the narrow tower windows, dawn was already recoloring the black sky to a dark blue. The troops battling to take the remaining courtyards were visible now in the dim morning light. Sir Weyd watched the dragon swooping on the King's troops as they fought the trolls. He noted that the beast seemed to care little whether he ravaged trolls as well.

As Weyd and his knights dragged Chastain's limp body out onto the battlement wall, the dragon once again took an amused perch upon the east tower. Sir Weyd knew then that the creature would not come to Chastain's aid. The dragon loved destruction for destruction's sake and cared not a bit for the welfare of those who followed him.

With the blast of a trumpet, the knights on the battlement called attention to themselves and their prisoner, who hung from ropes tied over the wall's crenels.

"You trolls," announced Sir Weyd. "Your master is in our hands. Lay down your arms now or you will suffer the same fate as he." The captain slapped Chastain's face in hopes of waking him. He fervently desired that the sorcerer be conscious to suffer every slice upon his body, but it was no use. They could not rouse him.

Weyd lifted his sword, savoring the anticipation of inflicting the first blow to Chastain. He cursed when his downward slice was interrupted by a mighty earthquake that nearly threw him from the battlement. He clung to the crenels to keep from falling to his death as the wrenching force shook. The walls cracked and stone fell away like a facade leaving a castle of massive crystal blocks that glowed with light from the fiery sunrise.

The dragon writhed screeching into the cloudless sky, and then with snorts of rage he flew away. From the east tower someone approached Sir Weyd on the glowing battlement.

"This is more of the sorcerer's trickery, no doubt!" exclaimed Sir Brin in disbelief at the approaching figure.

"No," Sir Weyd blinked as if to clear his eyesight and then stared again at the person coming toward them. "No, it is the Great King!" Sheathing his sword as he ran, Weyd was the first to reach the King and robustly embrace him. A cheer rose up from the watching army as the Great King clasped and greeted his captains on the battlement. The trolls laid down their arms to stare in awe at the King whose death they had witnessed.

"Sire, use my sword to finish Chastain," Weyd offered, seeing that the King had no weapon.

"There will be no execution," answered the King. "Chastain is no longer an enemy. After he spent his rage on me and thought he had won, he was finally able to see his true adversary. He is smitten not by some trance, but by his own deep grief over who he has become. So his restoration begins."

"Surely, you do not intend to forgive him!" protested Weyd incredulously.

"The curse of the dragon is now broken for all of you," announced the King. "There will be no execution. Have you not had your fill of death?"

The captains nodded slowly as they struggled to relinquish their yearning for Chastain's blood. Walking past them, the Great King lowered the unconscious sorcerer to lay at his feet and then kneeled to gently loosen the ropes from Chastain's wrists.

○   ○   ○

Personal Reflection

The Curse

✍ Parts of the parable that touched me are . . .

✍ When I read these parts I felt . . .

✍ Similar situations in my life are . . .

Each of us has a capacity for good and a capacity for evil. We each have a part within us like Chastain. In the space below, draw a picture showing the struggle between your "good" and "bad" sides. Don't worry about artistic ability or think too hard about this. Just sketch freely.

What or who brings out your evil side?

✍ _____

_____

Who does it attack?

✍ _____

What strengths would your dark side have if it were redeemed into health?

✍ _____

_____

o   o   o

We have traveled together in this land for a time now. My hope is that you have found much to help you as you continue traveling.

These next pages are for you to write a fairy tale about your life. Don't worry about spelling or grammar. Allow your imagination to roam. Are you a prince, an elf, or one of the fairy folk? What was it like where you grew up? Was there evil in your childhood from a troll, a wicked witch, a dragon, or something else? What have the major conflicts in your personal growth been? What have you been searching for in your life? Include an ending about how your quest will be resolved, even if you haven't experienced that ending yet.

Once upon a time . . .

_____

_____

_____

_____

_____

_____

_____

$\mathcal{A}$ PPENDIX 1

Support Group or Twelve-Step Group Journeys with the Parables

The parables can be used for a change of pace in an existing support group or therapy group. Or a group can be formed specifically for personal growth by going through the parables.

Suggested Group Format

1 to 1½ hours

1. Read a parable together so that it is freshly experienced.

a. Ask for three volunteers to read the parable aloud to the group (takes ten minutes or less). They take turns reading about a third of each page. Or select one volunteer to read the full parable.

or

b. Set aside ten minutes for the group members to read the parable silently. You may wish to play some pleasant background music during this time.

or

c. Alternate reading aloud one week, silently the next, and so on.

Even if participants read the parable before the group meets, it is best to set aside time to reexperience the parable at the beginning of each meeting. Feelings are then fresh for interacting with and discussing the reflections.

2. Reflections

Allow group members ten minutes to individually write in the parable's reflection section. You may wish to play some pleasant background music here also. Tell group members when two minutes of this time is left.

3. Small Group Sharing

(15 minutes for a 1 hour group; 30 minutes for a 1½ hour group)

Divide into groups of five or fewer people if the group is large. Share your thoughts and feelings about the parable, reflection, and your life. Announce when two minutes of this time is left. If possible, the small groups should divide up with the same people each week to allow for a deeper level of sharing.

4. Large Group Sharing

(15 minutes for a 1 hour group. 30 minutes for a 1½ hour group)

Gather together as a large group again with chairs in a circle. The more we hear others share, the more we learn about ourselves.

Guidelines for Sharing*

Read aloud just before the group divides into smaller circles for sharing.

- Allow everyone to share, answering one question at a time.
- Until everyone has shared, please don't crosstalk. ("Crosstalk" is when two people enter into a dialogue that excludes other group members.)
- No one has to share if they do not wish to.
- Please limit your comments or observations to your own personal experience.
- To the best of your ability, honestly share from your heart and not just from your head. Share the feelings you experienced from the parable and the reflection about your own life (for example, joy, sadness, anger, love, guilt, hurt, loneliness).
- Be supportive without giving advice.
- Refrain from criticizing or defending other group members.
- Take responsibility for yourself rather than try to fix others.
- What you hear about the personal lives of others is confidential; please leave it at this meeting.

* Adapted from Friends in Recovery, *The Twelve Steps: A Spiritual Journey* (San Diego, CA: Recovery Publications, 1988), pp. 160–172.

Other Options to Consider for Group Formats

1. Open or Closed Group?

- Open group—open to anyone who wishes to attend from week to week.
- Closed group—members are the same each week and have made a commitment to attend regularly.

Oftentimes a closed group will be open for the first two or three weeks so that people can decide if they wish to commit to it regularly. At each of those initial meetings, it is announced that the group will be closed after a certain date and will not accept new members.

2. Number of Group Meetings

- 19 week group—this time frame would allow for the completion of the entire book doing one parable a week.
- 6 week group—the first six parables ending with "Mirror, Mirror" are recommended for those desiring a shorter experience.

Groups usually meet once a week, but you may wish to schedule your meetings every other week or once a month. Some casual groups of friends going through the parables prefer a lighter schedule instead of a weekly support group.

3. Size of Group

If the group is larger than ten people, it is important to schedule time for the small group sharing with five or fewer people in each group. Otherwise there will not be enough time for everyone to share who would like to.

4. Role-Playing

During the large group sharing you may wish to ask for volunteers to act out a key portion of the parable for one or two minutes. No dialogue is needed for this. Some examples:

- "The Dragon"—The prince with villagers pointing accusing fingers at him.
- "Lady in Waiting"—A woman serving food to demanding guests around her table. She takes no time to sit down and eat for herself.
- "Dragon Flight"—The prince deciding between the dragon at the window and the Great King at the doorway.

Afterward the volunteers can share how they felt during the role-play and other group members can talk about how they felt watching it.

Sample Group Announcement

Personal Growth Group
19 Weeks

We will be going on an inner journey with the book *Parables for Personal Growth*. Issues explored include self-defeating behavior, codependency, inner child work, boundaries, depression, self-concept, loss of childhood, recovery from childhood abuse, dysfunctional family interactions, fears, anxiety, victimization by unhealthy groups, forgiveness and letting go, loss and grief.

The parables take place in a mythical realm not far from your own inner struggles. A noble prince who falls under the sway of a destructive dragon allows you to feel the process of recovery from self-defeating behavior. In another parable, an enchanted mirror leads a princess to mistakenly believe she is grotesque until she finally discovers her true identity.

These parables help us see our wounds and embrace healing truth into the brokenness. Each week we will discuss one parable, explore that struggle in our own lives, and support one another in moving forward.

Location: **Time:**

Group coordinator(s):   **Dates:**

Phone for more information:

(Include information about whether this will be an open or closed group.)

o   o   o

Twelve-Step Group

In addition to the reflection questions at the end of each parable you may wish to explore:

• Which of the Twelve Steps do you see in the parable?
• How does this character's struggle help you work a step in your own life?

$\mathcal{A}$ PPENDIX 2

The Twelve Steps of Recovery

1. We admitted we were powerless over people, substances, and things—that our lives had become unmanageable.
2. Came to believe that a Power greater than ourselves could restore us to sanity.
3. Made a decision to turn our will and our lives over to the care of God.
4. Made a searching and fearless moral inventory of ourselves.
5. Admitted to God, to ourselves, and to another human being the exact nature of our wrongs.
6. Were entirely ready to have God remove all these defects of character.
7. Humbly asked Him to remove our shortcomings.
8. Made a list of all persons we had harmed, and became willing to make amends to them all.
9. Made direct amends to such people wherever possible, except when to do so would injure them or others.
10. Continued to take personal inventory and when we were wrong, promptly admitted it.
11. Sought through prayer and meditation to improve our conscious contact with God, praying only for knowledge of His will for us and the power to carry that out.
12. Having had a spiritual awakening as the result of these steps, we tried to carry this message to others and to practice these principles in all our affairs.

The Twelve Steps of Alcoholics Anonymous°

1. We admitted we were powerless over alcohol—that our lives had become unmanageable.
2. Came to believe that a Power greater than ourselves could restore us to sanity.
3. Made a decision to turn our will and our lives over to the care of God *as we understood Him*.
4. Made a searching and fearless moral inventory of ourselves.
5. Admitted to God, to ourselves, and to another human being the exact nature of our wrongs.
6. Were entirely ready to have God remove all these defects of character.
7. Humbly asked Him to remove our shortcomings.
8. Made a list of all persons we had harmed, and became willing to make amends to them all.
9. Made direct amends to such people wherever possible, except when to do so would injure them or others.
10. Continued to take personal inventory and when we were wrong, promptly admitted it.
11. Sought through prayer and meditation to improve our conscious contact with God, *as we understood Him*, praying only for knowledge of His will for us and the power to carry that out.
12. Having had a spiritual awakening as the result of these steps, we tried to carry this message to alcoholics, and to practice these principles in all our affairs.

$\mathcal{R}$ E S O U R C E S

Books

ADULT CHILDREN FROM DYSFUNCTIONAL FAMILIES

Bradshaw, John. *Bradshaw: On the Family*. Deerfield Beach, FL: Health Communications, Inc., 1988.

Coleman, Sally, and Rita J. Donley. *Life Work: A Workbook for Adult Children of Alcoholics*. Minneapolis, MN: CompCare, 1992.

Friends in Recovery. *The 12 Steps for Adult Children*. San Diego, CA: Recovery Publications, 1987.

Gil, Eliana. *Outgrowing the Pain*. New York: Dell, 1988.

Kritsberg, Wayne. *The Adult Children of Alcoholics Syndrome*. New York: Bantam, 1988.

Ross, Ron. *When I Grow Up I Want to Be an Adult*. San Diego, CA: Recovery Publications, 1990.

ADULTS MOLESTED AS CHILDREN

Davis, Laura. *The Courage to Heal Workbook: For Women and Men Survivors of Child Sexual Abuse*. New York: Harper & Row, 1990.

Frank, Jan. *A Door of Hope*. San Bernardino, CA: Here's Life Publishers, 1987.

Graber, Ken. *Ghosts in the Bedroom: A Guide for Partners of Incest Survivors*. Deerfield Beach, FL: Health Communications, 1991.

Hunter, Mic. *Abused Boys: The Neglected Victims of Sexual Abuse.* Lexington, MA: Lexington Books, 1990.

Lew, Mike. *Victims No Longer: Men Recovering from Incest and Other Sexual Child Abuse.* New York: Harper & Row, 1990.

Love, Patricia. *The Emotional Incest Syndrome.* New York: Bantam Books, 1991.

Maltz, Wendy. *The Sexual Healing Journey.* New York: HarperCollins, 1991.

Sanders, Timothy. *Male Survivors: 12-Step Recovery Program for Survivors of Childhood Sexual Abuse.* Freedom, CA: The Crossing Press, 1991.

ANXIETY

Weekes, Claire. *Hope and Help for Your Nerves.* New York: Bantam Books, 1978.
———. *More Help for Your Nerves.* New York: Bantam, 1987.

CODEPENDENCY

Beattie, Melody. *Beyond Codependency.* New York: Harper/Hazelden, 1989.
———. *Codependent No More.* New York: Harper/Hazelden, 1987.

DEPRESSION AND SUICIDE

Beattie, Melody, ed. *A Reason to Live.* Wheaton, IL: Tyndale House, 1991.

Copeland, Mary Ellen. *The Depression Workbook.* Oakland, CA: New Harbinger Publications, 1992.

Quinnett, Paul. *Suicide: The Forever Decision.* New York: Continuum Publishing, 1987.

FORGIVENESS AND LETTING GO

Augsburger, David. *Caring Enough to Forgive: Caring Enough to Not Forgive.* Scottdale, PA: Herald Press, 1981.

Smedes, Lewis. *Forgive and Forget.* San Francisco: Harper & Row, 1984.

GRIEF

Colgrove, Melba, Harold Bloomfield, and Peter McWilliams. *How to Survive the Loss of a Love.* Los Angeles, CA: Prelude Press, 1976, 1991.

Deits, Bob. *Life After Loss.* Tucson, AZ: Fisher Books, 1988.

Heavilin, Marilyn Willett. *When Your Dreams Die.* San Bernadino, CA: Here's Life Publishers, 1990.

James, John W., and Frank Cherry. *The Grief Recovery Handbook*. New York: Harper & Row, 1988.

Lewis, C. S. *A Grief Observed*. London: Faber & Faber, 1961.

HIGHER POWER

Dawson, John. *The Father Heart of God*. Available for $.06 from Last Days Ministries, Box 40, Lindale, TX 75771–0040. Ask for pamphlet LD#46.

Lewis, C. S. *The Lion, the Witch and the Wardrobe*. New York: Collier Books, 1970. (Book one in the Chronicles of Narnia.)
————. *Mere Christianity*. New York: Macmillan, 1960.

INNER CHILD

Biffle, Christopher. *A Journey Through Your Childhood*. Los Angeles: Tarcher, 1989.

Bradshaw, John. *Homecoming: Reclaiming and Championing Your Inner Child*. New York: Bantam Books, 1990.

Capacchione, Lucia. *Recovery of Your Inner Child & the Creative Journal*. P.O. Box 5805, Santa Monica, CA 90409. (213) 281–7495. Simon & Schuster/Fireside © 1991.

Pollard, John K. *Self Parenting*. Malibu, CA: Generic Human Studies Publishing, 1987.

SELF-CONCEPT

McDowell, Josh. *Building Your Self Image*. Wheaton, IL: Tyndale House, 1988.

Roever, Dave. *Welcome Home, Davey*. Waco, TX: Word Books, 1986.

TWELVE STEPS WORKBOOKS

Carnes, Patrick. *A Gentle Path Through the Twelve Steps: For All People in the Process of Recovery*. Minneapolis, MN: CompCare, 1989.

Friends in Recovery. *The Twelve Steps: A Spiritual Journey*. San Diego, CA: Recovery Publications, 1988.
————. *The Twelve Steps: A Way Out*. San Diego, CA: Recovery Publications, 1987.

Weinberg, Jon with Daryl Kosloske. *Fourth Step Guide: Journey into Growth*. Minneapolis, MN: Compcare, 1977.

Wills-Brandon, Carla. *The Fourth Step: Examining Your Childhood Survival Skills*. Deerfield, FL: Health Communications, Inc.

RELIGIOUS OR PSYCHOTHERAPY CULT VICTIMIZATION

California State Department of Consumer Affairs. *Professional Therapy Never Includes Sex* (1990). $.50 a copy from Office of Procurement, Publications Section, P. O. Box 1015, North Highlands, CA 95660.

Fischer, Kathleen. "Abuse of Therapeutic Techniques Harms Public." *American Psychological Association Monitor* (April 1985): 7.

Johnson, David, and Jeff VanVonderen. *The Subtle Power of Spiritual Abuse.* Minneapolis, MN: Bethany House, 1991.

Meacham, Andrew. "Losing Your Soul to a Cult." *Changes* (September/October 1989): 28.

Singer, Margaret Thaler, Maurice K. Termerlin, and Michael D. Langhone. "Psychotherapy Cults." *Cultic Studies Journal* 7(1991): 101–25.

V., Patricia. "The Co-Dependent Sponsor." *Changes* (March–April 1991): 52–59. (The differences between healthy and controlling Twelve Step sponsoring relationships.)

Support Groups, Hotlines, Referral Sources

The following addresses may help you to get in touch with a local chapter:

Adult Children of Alcoholics,
Central Service Board
P.O. Box 35623
Los Angeles, CA 90035
(213) 464-4423

Al-Anon/Alateen
Family Group Headquarters
P.O. Box 182
Madison Square Station
New York, NY 10159
(800) 344-2666
(212) 302-7240

Alcoholics Anonymous
P.O. Box 459
Grand Central Station
New York, NY 10163
(212) 686-1100

American Family Foundation
P.O. Box 2265
Bonita Springs, FL 33959-2265
(212) 249-7693
Research, information, publications for cult victims.

Childhelp USA Child Abuse Hotline
(800) 422–4453.

Cult Awareness Network
(C.A.N.—affiliates nationwide)
National Office
2421 West Pratt Blvd. #1173
Chicago, IL 60645
(312) 267–7777
Catalog of helpful information and referrals to support groups.

Debtors Anonymous
314 West 53rd Street
New York, NY 10018
(212) 969-0710

Emotions Anonymous
P.O. Box 4245
St. Paul, MN 55104
(612) 647-9712

Exodus International
P.O. Box 2121
San Rafael, CA 94912
(415) 454-1017
FAX (415) 454-7826
Network of Christian organizations that help homosexuals seeking a change in lifestyle. Support groups.

Gamblers Anonymous
P.O. Box 17173
Los Angeles, CA 90017
(213) 386-8769

Incest Survivors Anonymous
P.O. Box 5613
Long Beach, CA 90800

Narcotics Anonymous,
World Service Office
16155 Wyandotte Street
Van Nuys, CA 91406
(818) 780-3951

National Association
for Children of Alcoholics
31582 Coast Highway, Suite B
South Laguna, CA 92677
(714) 499-3889

**National Association
for Christian Recovery**
P.O. Box 11095
Whittier, CA 90603
(310) 697-6201
Referrals, magazine, conferences.

**National Clearinghouse
for Alcohol Information**
P.O. Box 1908
Rockville, MD 20850

National Suicide Prevention Hotline
(800) 333-4444.

**North American Society
of Adlerian Psychology**
65 East Wacker Place #400
Chicago, IL 60601-7203
(312) 629-8801
Referrals to Adlerian psychotherapists.

**Overeaters Anonymous,
World Service Office**
2190 190th Street
Torrance, CA 90504
(213) 542-8363

Parents Anonymous
(800) 421–0353.
Free anonymous consultation, professional help, support groups for parenting issues including child abuse.

Sex Addicts Anonymous
Twin Cities S.A.A.
P.O. Box 3038
Minneapolis, MN 53403
(213) 386-8789

Spender Menders
P.O. Box 15000-156
San Francisco, CA 94115
(415) 773-9754

You can find Twelve Step programs in your local telephone directory:

A.A.—Alcoholics Anonymous
Al–Anon—Family and Friends of Alcoholics
A.C.O.A.—Adult Children of Alcoholics
C.A.—Cocaine Anonymous
E.H.A.—Emotional Health Anonymous
F.A.—Families Anonymous (Family and friends of drug users)
G.A.—Gamblers Anonymous
I.S.A.—Incest Survivors Anonymous
N.A.—Narcotics Anonymous
Nar-Anon—Family and Friends of Substance Abusers
O.A.—Overeaters Anonymous
P.A.—Parents Anonymous, for parents who may endanger their children
S.A.A.—Sex Addicts Anonymous
Spender Menders—for those with a spending addiction